D0717442

itv SPORT

LEWIS HAMILTON

Bruce Jones

itv SPORT

LEWIS HAMILTON

Bruce Jones

CARLTON
BOOKS

First published in 2007 by
Carlton Books Limited,
20 Mortimer Street,
London W1T 3JW

10 9 8 7 6 5 4 3 2 1

A CIP catalogue record for this book is available from the British Library.

ISBN: 978-1-84442-027-8

Project Director: Matthew Lowing
Designer: David Etherington
Editorial: John Behan
Picture Research: Paul Langan
Production: Lisa Cook

Printed in Italy

CONTENTS

INTRODUCTION

"Rookie driver turns on the style", "rookie driver takes on the world champion," "rookie driver held back on the streets of Monaco" and "rookie driver turns winner" are headlines that have been emblazoned on the sports pages, front pages even, of newspapers around the world in Lewis Hamilton's first season of Formula One. No first year Formula One racing driver has ever made such an impact. With the wins flowing from June onwards, when he broke his duck in Montreal, Lewis established himself as the leader. This wasn't subterfuge, it was blatant leading from the front. Lewis has been outstanding. He has revitalised the sport, he has become a role model and he gives the feeling that this is just the beginning of a trajectory that will make him to motor racing what world-beater Tiger Woods is to golf.

Already the pressure is mounting, with expectations so high that his yellow crash helmet is always the one to look for as the pack of 22 Formula One cars accelerates in tight packs down to the first corner of a grand prix and his silver and dayglo orange McLaren is expected to be first to the finish line. Even on days when not everything went right, or the rival Ferrari team got everything right to assume control, Lewis would finish on the podium, making remarkably few mistakes even when under pressure and shattering records as he went. No Formula One rookie had ever been so successful, no career has ever looked so bright. It's true, too, that no other driver has ever subsumed the rest of the field into also-rans where the media are concerned. For 2007 at least, Lewis Hamilton is Formula One. It's extraordinary and, plainly, it's unsustainable, but there can be no doubting that this is the start of a very special Formula One career. Quite what its parameters will contain is impossible to guess, but he's with one of the top two teams and making hay while the sun shines in such a way that suggests that Lewis will be in a top team for years to come. The records are there to be broken. Before people get too carried away, however, he is half a decade of wins worth away from Michael Schumacher's dominant standard of 91, so there's a long, long way to go.

Like many words describing excellence, prodigy can be overused, being apportioned to some who are merely good rather than great. Undeniably, Wolfgang

» A year ago, only dyed-in-the-wool motor racing fans recognised this profile. Now, Lewis Hamilton is on the way to becoming one of the world's most famous sportsmen.

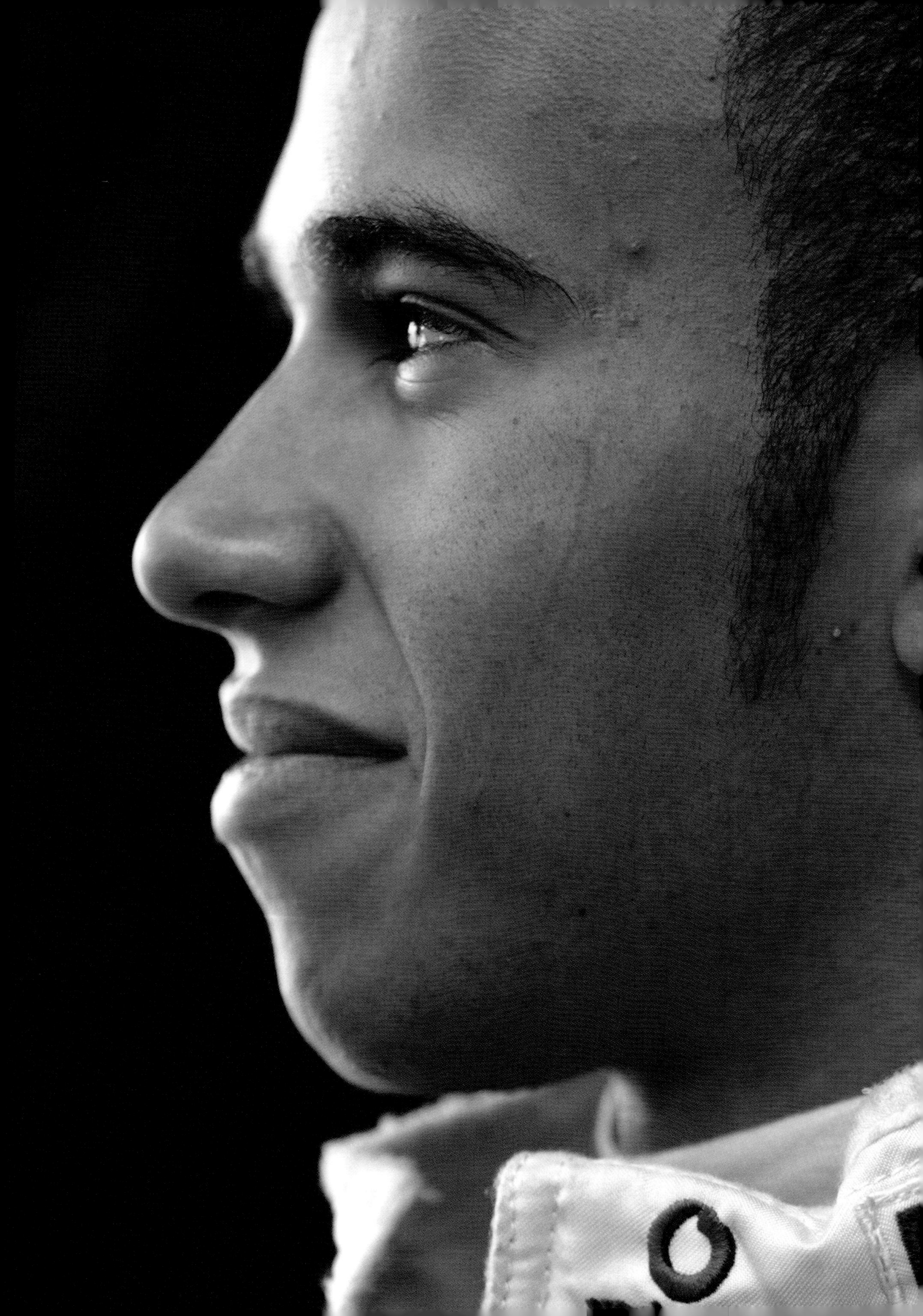

Lewis the schoolboy racer was something that could only happen if Lewis met his side of a deal with his father Anthony that his studying must not be neglected.

“When I was young, some of the stars signed autographs without even looking at me. I’ll never do that.” *Lewis Hamilton*

Amadeus Mozart was a child prodigy, composing music by the tender age of five. Against this, Lewis Carl Hamilton was something of a slow starter, although by any other term of reference he was a trailblazer, an example to others, with eye-to-hand co-ordination that set him apart from his contemporaries. This and a will to win that was passed directly from his father Anthony. To whit, Lewis was beating adult radio-controlled car racers by the time he was seven.

That his parents wanted Lewis to be a child of world-beating potential could actually have been detected far earlier, as they were so impressed by multiple Olympic gold medal winner Carl Lewis that they simply transposed the American athlete’s names when naming their son.

There can be no doubting that values are extremely important in the Hamilton household and the fact that they all stick to them is testament to the way that they have been applied. The family are exceptionally close, with the Anthony/Lewis, father/son relationship the most important dynamic in Lewis’s life. It’s the driving force behind every step that he has taken and every hurdle that he has cleared. Their climb to the top of the tree has certainly not been without struggle, as money was incredibly tight in the early days of his kart racing career, but they are all the stronger for this. Lewis and Anthony’s journey has undoubtedly not been one of privilege, but one of focus and dedication, to say nothing of Lewis’s ability being fine-tuned into once-in-a-generation skill by incredible self-discipline and no little denial of the things that teenagers like to do. His passage to the top has been about looking, learning and applying and, ultimately, about maximising all the opportunities that came along once the McLaren Formula One team took its vital mentoring role.

Racing great Sir Stirling Moss – a man who certainly can identify talent when he sees it – is of the opinion that Lewis is the best-prepared driver ever to reach Formula One and in this lies the secret to the way that Lewis hit the ground running when he made his debut in the Australian Grand Prix at Melbourne’s Albert Park circuit in March. It showed how Lewis did more than just take McLaren’s money for the nine years since they signed him when he was just a 13-year-old kartist. He had honed his race skills, certainly, but he had maximised everything in his approach to racing, learned as many lessons as he could about chassis set-

“Lewis has been trained all the way up the ladder, and he’s taken it all on board.” *F1 champion Sir Jackie Stewart*

up and data analysis, about the rules and regulations and also trained himself to be in peak fitness for this sapping job. Lewis is also a natural with the media, although his debut season has been marked by McLaren holding him on a tight rein and keeping the media at bay. This has been frustrating for those wanting to write stories about him, but as Lewis has made himself *the* story of the season, the hottest story in Formula One for years, the driver who was putting the interest back in a sport that had had it taken away by years of domination by Michael Schumacher, and the man who turned Formula One from all-white to multi-cultural, it was annoying but it made sense as Lewis needed to be allowed to focus on the driving.

What has shone through, though, apart form his racer’s instinct, is how normal a person Lewis is, how natural in all circumstances with a welcome lack of “front”.

Indeed, Anthony has always kept Lewis’s feet on the ground. Even when Lewis was already world kart champion, the youngest ever as it happens, he made sure that he was out working in any down time to keep instilling the value of work. This was in the valet bay of the local Mercedes dealership that had supplied him with a car to get him to races after McLaren Mercedes had agreed to help financially with his career. Lewis’s meticulous approach made his work stand out, which is just how Anthony liked it and it certainly left a mark on his work mates who recall him as a down-to-earth individual who was clearly going to go a long way in whatever he did in life. They weren’t wrong.

One of the keys to Lewis’s early years is that Anthony was good, make that exceptionally good, at pushing Lewis forward. He put in considerable legwork to keep the show on the road and Lewis could not be other than impressed by his family’s sacrifices. He was also fortunate that Anthony didn’t fit the mould of the “karting dad”, the sort who will scream at his child for failing to win and curse at anyone who prevents him from doing so. Best of all, Anthony has always asked for advice and taken heed of it.

Anthony told *The Independent* newspaper that the family had always tried to bring Lewis up to do things right and to understand that positive consequences flow from taking an honest approach to things.

From the day he proved an instant hit in Formula One, the media have followed Lewis's every move.

Lewis himself attributes much of his success to the single-minded maxim of never giving up, in any circumstances, saying: "When the going gets tough, just keep on pushing. That's what I always do." Some of his greatest races, when he has had to fight his way from the back to the front, such as at the second GP2 race at Istanbul in 2006, give credence to that.

It's not just all a matter of guts and application though, and many of the sport's keenest insiders eulogise over Lewis's driving style, with his wide entry line, his smooth delivery and his ability to carry momentum through corners, even with the tail of the car out of line. To those with a less trained eye, those less able to understand the dynamics of a fast lap, Lewis's results are enough to convince them of his merits.

When it comes to gauging how good any top driver is, it makes the most sense to listen to the greats. Sir Stirling Moss is one such as the greatest driver never to become world champion, and he is so excited by Lewis's talents that he is happy to compare his skills to his own teacher: five-time world champion Juan Manuel Fangio who was able to adapt to any machine in any conditions and still be fast. Moss goes further, though, telling journalist Paul Fearnley: "In any era, there are four or five drivers with a realistic chance of winning, and Lewis became one of them straight away. I was a racer, and I think he's one too. He's not only fast, just look at some of his overtaking manoeuvres."

Sir Jackie Stewart is also a staunch supporter: "A real weakness within Formula One is that hardly any drivers believe that they need coaching," explains the three-time world champion. "Lewis is different. He has been coached all the way up the ladder and he's taken it all on board." Stewart, an individual of remarkable perception, goes on to say that the majority of racing drivers are lethargic about everything outside the cockpit, but he was impressed that Lewis could all but recite the rule book back at him. In a sport in which success can be

Lewis's success in Formula One is about more than his natural speed and competitive instinct, with the knowledge that McLaren has imbued being a vital ingredient.

measured by thousandths of a second, every little counts, and the last driver to bother to harness all those extra little increments went on to collect seven Formula One titles. He was, of course, Michael Schumacher.

Throughout his career, the issue of Lewis's colour has been regarded as an extra, as a bonus rather than as the reason for his trajectory to the top, which is refreshing. It would take a madman to suggest that the reason that he has been groomed by McLaren for success is tokenism. Put plainly, the stopwatch doesn't lie: Lewis is an exceptional driver full stop. That he is black and successful will undoubtedly add new fans to the sport, but possibly not as many as those attracted simply by a new talent of world-beating potential. In the post-Michael Schumacher years, racing fans are keen for a new hero, and preferably one more accessible than Michael, one too with a better judgment on what is fair in battle. In short, Lewis is already a role-model of considerable appeal.

Speed and dedication aside, one of the most appealing attributes that Lewis displays is that he seems unchanged by success and the accompanying, new-found fame, remaining open and honest whenever confronted by microphone or autograph-seeking fan. Long may he stay so. Indeed, Lewis has clear ideas of why he must always remain accessible. "When I was young," said Lewis, "some of the stars of the day signed autographs without even looking at me. I'll never do that and always look children in the eye when I sign autographs for them. It's important." Too right, and so far he has practiced what he preaches, although his right arm really must have ached after the build-up to the British GP.

Just staying as Lewis will be increasingly hard, although Lewis's family will keep him in check, even when the exponential skew on his life from becoming one of the world's most recognisable faces will certainly make this increasingly hard. Lewis said when he was thronged by thousands at the Goodwood Festival of Speed at the end of June that it was getting harder to go around without being recognised, but that he still tried to go out to the cinema, as he had before. So, if you're in Woking and spot an athletic person of Lewis's build heading for the flicks, with head angled down and face covered by the peak of a cap, give him some peace.

Bruce Jones, October 2007

Pi Research
3

CHAPTER 1
CHILDHOOD PROTEGE & KARTING

"I went up to Anthony and asked him how many races Lewis had done. He amazed me when he said one."

Kart boss Martin Hines

CHILDHOOD PROTEGE & KARTING

» You might see a sweet, gap-toothed little boy on a kart, but had you spoken to Lewis the cadet karter you would soon have realised his determination to win.

All babies are precious, but Lewis was an extremely precious baby when he was born in Tewin near Stevenage, Hertfordshire to Carmen and Anthony Hamilton on 7 January 1985, as they had spent years trying for a child. Sadly, his parents separated when Lewis was just two, with Lewis staying on with his mother on the Shephall estate. Theirs was an end-of-terrace council house and there was nothing to suggest that his life would be heading for the stars, destined for universal fame and untold wealth. Indeed, life was tough for Lewis in those early years, with no frills.

The number one passion in Lewis's childhood was cars and Anthony bought him a radio-controlled car that he was soon racing with prodigious ability. Such was his prowess, that Lewis was invited to appear on the BBC's *Blue Peter* children's television programme in 1992, on which he wiped the floor with his adult rivals. It might have appeared as a novelty, something of a trick to have a tiny seven-year-old performing with such aplomb, but the skill was there, that innate sense of co-ordination and balance that is possessed by all top sportsmen and women. It would be another year until Lewis found another outlet for his uncanny ability, karts, but until then he carried on as a normal schoolboy, blending in with the crowd as much as possible.

A teacher from his primary school, Peartree Spring Infant School in Stevenage, recalls Lewis first and foremost as a smiley and well-mannered boy rather than as a hard-nosed competitor. "He was a bright little button," said former headteacher Carol Hopkins, "but normal, very normal."

Although popular with the teachers, it wasn't all easy going at primary school, however, as Lewis suffered from bullying at school, perhaps for being different, for being black. To combat this, he took up karate and, typically, went on to gain an intermediate black belt.

This was indicative of the work ethos instilled in him by his father. Anthony's family had come to Britain from Grenada in the 1950s, with his father Davidson looking to set the family

LEWIS HAMILTON

Fresh-faced but already attracting sponsorship, Lewis became one to watch in karting almost from his very first race. This is Lewis, aged 12, in 1997.

“Lewis was a bright little button But normal, very normal.”

Headteacher Carol Hopkins

on the road to a better life by working on the railways. That push to succeed was certainly passed down to Anthony and, in turn, to Lewis, particularly once his mother Carmen decided to quit Tewin for London when Lewis was 10 and so he moved in with his father, his stepmother Linda and stepbrother Nicolas.

Another influence on Lewis is the way that stepbrother Nicolas remains cheerful in the face of a major handicap: he has cerebral palsy. Indeed, Nicolas is already a popular member of the F1 paddock and Lewis calls him his biggest inspiration. There are six years between them, with Nicolas just 16, but they are as close as brothers can be, with Lewis spending much of his down time back at home, challenging Nicolas on assorted racing computer games.

As fate would have it, one of the country's leading kart circuits, Rye House, was just around the corner in Hoddesdon and it was here that Anthony took Lewis in 1993, when he was eight, for a visit that would shape the rest of his life.

Cadet class racing is the bottom rung of the ladder, the category in which children can start racing once they turn eight. Powered by 60cc engines, there is a minimum weight for kart and driver combined and an upper age limit for participants of 12. Lewis, still under four foot tall at the time, was straight into the thick of the action in 1993, very much the cat among the pigeons. Novices are identified by racing with black plates on their kart for their first six races and it's rare to see them anywhere near the sharp end of the field, yet this is where Lewis spent his races right from day one.

Martin Hines – former Superkart racing World Champion, boss of Britain's leading kart manufacturer Zip Kart and effective godfather of British kart racing for the past two decades – was a fan of Lewis's right from the very beginning. “I was there at Lewis's very first race at Rye House, as I was at the track running karts for my son Luke and Gary Paffett that day. We watched Lewis progress through the day and reckoned that he'd done really well as a novice. I went up to his father Anthony afterwards and asked him how many races Lewis had done. He amazed me when he said ‘one’, which made Lewis's speed even more impressive. So I told Anthony to come to my factory the next day as it was just down the road from them in

"The sort of raw talent to take a driver to F1 is rare. There are only one or two a generation who are that good." *Circuit owner Bill Sisley*

Hoddesdon, and we got involved from there, giving technical and financial assistance as he drove our karts from then on."

Bill Sisley, managing director of the Buckmore Park kart circuit in Kent, was also sold on Lewis from the first day that he saw him race: "I have talent-spotted for 35 years and have always said that I can tell within two laps whether a young driver has what it takes, but the sort of raw talent that is enough to take them all the way to F1 is rare. There are only one or two in a generation who are that good. Lewis was one of them and his talent shouted out."

The cadet champion that year was Michael Spencer, who was a couple of years older than Lewis. "It was a tough year," Spencer recalls, "but I don't remember Lewis much, as it tends to take a year or so before drivers find their feet and I'd moved on before the 1995 season when he won the title. I actually remember Lewis much better from when we raced in Formula A in Europe in 2000."

Spencer raced on successfully through the kart ranks, becoming British Junior then Senior champion. He graduated to car racing and won the Zip Formula title in 2002 before racing against Lewis again in Formula Renault in 2003 when he showed flashes of form to end up eighth overall. But then, like so many others, he dropped out of racing due to a lack of money and he's now looking after the karting careers of brothers Mark and Tom Bowmer, while competing himself in the British Open series.

Back for a second season of cadet karting in 1994, Niki Richardson raced to the title ahead of future touring car and British GT racer Luke Hines, but Lewis was increasingly competitive as he and Anthony developed together as a team, with son driving and father having to get to grips with the exacting task of making sure that Lewis's kart hit the track in a competitive condition. This could have led to tensions, but both were focused enough to realise that they were working towards a common goal.

Still aged only 10, that's to say with as many as a further couple of years of cadet kart racing open to him, Lewis raced in cadet karts again in 1995, and he proved

» Success in the McClaren Mercedes Champions of the Future series is what propelled Lewis towards the top of karting, starting with his cadet title in 1996.

McLAREN MERC
HIGHLA
SPRI
NATURAL MIN
FORMULA
Zapelli
HIGHLAND
SPRING
Zapelli

“My dad can be really hard on me. But, at the end of the day, we’re a team and we’ll make it.”

Lewis Hamilton

Little Lewis at the *Autosport* Awards with Williams Formula One driver Jacques Villeneuve in December 1996, the night that he met Ron Dennis.

that all the faith shown in his ability was well founded as he became the youngest ever British champion, adding the STP Cadet championship title for good measure.

The year of 1995 also marked that other major landmark in his life, when his mother decided to move to London and Lewis elected, since karting was everything to him and Anthony was the one who made it happen, to stay on in Stevenage in a one-bedroomed flat... Lewis’s birthmother Carmen has since said that there was no way that she would have been able to raise the funds to keep Lewis’s adored karting career on track. Anthony was the mover and shaker in that department and so Lewis stayed with his father.

Knowing that he was going to have to do something different to earn more money to keep Lewis’s burgeoning karting career on track, Anthony chose this moment to take redundancy from his job at British Rail and so started his famous stint of holding down three jobs simultaneously just to pay the bills. This was a difficult period, with time at a premium as he drove Lewis all over the country to the races, but the wheels stayed on the wagon, just.

In 1996, McLaren fittingly took an interest in up-and-coming stars by sponsoring the McLaren Mercedes Champions of the Future series that had been instigated by Martin Hines. It stood out from other karting championships not just because it had the involvement of a top Formula One team, but because it was televised. This was where all aspiring kart stars wanted to do their winning, a never-before-seen shop-window for their talents and hopefully an arena in which they could attract sponsorship to help them advance up the motor racing ladder.

Lewis became cadet champion again, adding the Sky TV Kart Masters and Five Nations titles.

The television coverage also gave Lewis a chance to hone another facet of his portfolio: appearing in front of TV cameras. As a frequent race winner, there were plenty of interviews to do and thus plenty of opportunities to prove what a well-adjusted and natural young man he was, at the age of 11...

With the backing McLaren Mercedes, Lewis cut a swathe through the ranks of senior karting, all the way to becoming the youngest ever world number one.

JOE BLOGGS
JEANSWEAR
Pi Research

Lewis, still a cadet kart racer, poses with Niki Cleland, son of British Touring Car Champion John Cleland.

The PI Research logo on Lewis's visor identifies this as 1997, when Lewis stepped up from cadets to the more powerful Junior Yamaha class.

Television presenter and radio DJ David "Kid" Jensen was fronting the show and suggested that Lewis's name would one day be on the side of a Formula One car as he stood out not just for his speed but for his natural way that was always appealing, never arrogant.

This was also the year that Lewis moved up to secondary school, to the John Henry Newman Catholic School in Stevenage, where he again went quietly about his business, but was able to compare his sporting progress with that of another incredibly focused and talented class-mate, Ashley Young, who was soon being spotted by footballing scouts and is now starring for Aston Villa. Lewis also played midfield, but he realised that compared to Young his best hopes of hitting the top lay in four-wheeled sport rather than on the football field.

One of the key moments in Lewis's burgeoning career came that December, when Lewis made a major impression on a very important person when he attended the end-of-year *Autosport* Awards dinner at the Grosvenor House Hotel on London's Park Lane to collect a trophy. This VIP was McLaren principal Ron Dennis. On being asked later for his autograph and a drive with McLaren in the future, Dennis looked down, smiled and wrote into Lewis's autograph book "call me again in nine years." A few years later, though, it was Dennis who picked up the telephone, but more of that later...

Martin Hines takes up the story. "Lewis was on our table at the *Autosport* Awards as one of the McLaren Mercedes Champions of the Future title winners," reports the Zip Kart boss. "I took him, Gary (Paffett) – who had won the Senior McLaren Mercedes Champions of the Future title – and my son Luke up to speak to Ron [Dennis] after the presentations and suggested that he got them all under contract. Ten years later, both Lewis and Gary are McLaren drivers." Gary has been a test driver for McLaren since 2006.

McLaren Formula One team boss Ron Dennis poses with Lewis when he was a guest of the team at the 1997 Belgian Grand Prix at Spa-Francorchamps.

For 1997, as he was about to exceed the age limit for cadets, Lewis moved up to the Junior Yamaha class for racers aged between 12 and 16. Lewis took to these more powerful karts like a duck to water, racing to the McLaren Mercedes Champions of the Future and British Super One championship titles. Backed by Pi Research – a company owned by Tony Purnell who would go on to run Jaguar Racing in years to come – Lewis was soon in among the winners.

Lewis appeared on *Blue Peter* again and told viewers the following: "Racing against people older than me is quite a challenge as they know the tracks better than me and they've been racing longer, but I'm beating them." Others might have laughed at this moment, but Lewis was deadly serious. Kart racing was fun, but it wasn't a game to him. There wasn't room out on the track for sentiments, as Lewis went on to explain, saying: "I've got a lot of friends in karting, but when we're out on the track they're not my friends as I'm out to get them."

When quizzed about what it was like being run by his father, Lewis explained that this too meant running outside a child's normal comfort zone from time to time. "My Dad can be really hard on me," said Lewis. "When things aren't going to plan, he's even harder. But, at the end of the day, we're a team and we'll make it."

Anthony had clear ideas of why Lewis might just make it: "He's very determined and does not like losing. That's why he wins."

Win he did and Lewis kept on moving up, but ascending the rungs of the karting ladder means taking on more power, and this is what Lewis did when he stepped up to JICA (Junior Intercontinental A) in 1998. This meant that he would be racing a kart powered by a 100cc piston-ported engine in this extremely popular class for 13 to 16-year-olds. This was where karting would get really serious.

“Lewis is very determined and does not like losing. That’s why he wins.” *Anthony Hamilton*

Lewis really looks the part as he smiles for this publicity shot with his kart decked out in a livery to match the McLaren Mercedes Formula One cars.

“My ambition is to get to Formula One. I enjoy the speed and would like to be with all the big guys.”

Lewis Hamilton

The most important event related to 1998 was that Lewis landed support from the McLaren Mercedes Formula One team. Yes, the telephone call that McLaren boss Ron Dennis made came, offering to help with Lewis's career, with the end goal being Formula One. Of course reaching Formula One was Lewis's ambition too, but it seemed a long, long way off. Yet, here was the boss of the pre-eminent team offering to help get him there. It was almost unbelievable. Thus Lewis became the youngest ever driver contracted to a Formula One team and he would never race with equipment other than the best from then on.

The phone call came after Lewis and Andrew

Prince Charles looks suitably entertained by something that the 14-year-old Lewis has said to him when the Prince of Wales visited McLaren's headquarters in Woking.

Anthony is the proudest of fathers and every additional trophy added to Lewis's collection made clear to him that all of his sacrifices were worthwhile.

Delahunty – a winner of one of the previous year's McLaren Mercedes Champions of the Future titles – were taken to the Belgian Grand Prix as part of their prize. It was here at Spa-Francorchamps at the end of August 1997, seemingly, that Dennis decided that he really liked what he saw in Lewis. And then he made the telephone call early in 1998 that meant that Anthony, who was already holding down three jobs to finance Lewis's karting, might be able to back off a little. Indeed, Anthony was subsequently able to establish his own IT consultancy, from which he has since made a fortune. It shows that champions' genes are deep in the Hamilton DNA.

After the deal was done with McLaren Mercedes, Lewis told a television news reporter where he was heading: "My ambition is to get to Formula One. I enjoy the speed, and would like to be with all the big guys and to be making lots of money." The sentiments were clear, concise and focused, particularly as they were the words of a 13-year-old. Only now, in 2007, is there any inkling of just how much he might earn, with the sport's insiders talking of hundreds of millions of pounds.

Armed with this vital finance for his 1998 campaign, Anthony felt he should spend it wisely, to impress McLaren that he wasn't being profligate with their money. So he and Lewis followed the course taken by numerous champions before him, including David Coulthard, Anthony Davidson and Paffett, by signing to be a full member of Zip Kart's Young Guns team under the guidance of Martin Hines.

"You could say that Ron Dennis made Lewis, or I did by helping him in karts," said Hines, "but actually the only reason that Lewis is where he is today, winning grands prix for McLaren, is the little man behind the wheel: Lewis himself." said Hines.

"People ask me constantly what Lewis is like," Hines continues, "and I tell them that he's the same today as he was as a 10-year-old. They also ask whether he's cut out to take the

Lewis doing what he does best, racing at speed in the Intercontinental A class for Keke Rosberg's TeamMBM.com outfit in 1999. Lewis won that year's Italian title.

bm
5

MiR
Parilla
FM
AMG
L. Hamilton

“People ask me what Lewis is like and I tell them that he’s the same today as he was as a 10-year-old.” *Martin Hines*

pressure, but I can guarantee that a driver who has lined up as a 10-year-old in front of a television audience of millions having to win a race to secure a championship can cope with pressure. I don’t think it will ever get to Lewis.”

As always, even though Lewis was stepping up a category again, he proved the maxim that “class will out”, ending the 1998 season as the runner-up in the McLaren Mercedes Champions of the Future series behind Frazer Sheader, emphasising just how competitive he could be even against drivers who were several years older than him at a stage of life where a few years can seem like an eternity as puberty hits and leaves boys racing against young adults.

Lewis also started racing abroad in 1998, as Anthony wanted Lewis to take on the best of his contemporaries so that he could continue not only to learn his craft but also the circuits on which he’d need to shine if he was to work his way successfully through the senior kart categories in the years ahead before graduating to car racing. To this end, Anthony signed mechanic Kieran Crawley to look after him as he went off to race for TopKart, for whom Zip Kart is the British distributor. With Lewis being only 13 years old, Kieran also had to act as his chaperone when Anthony wasn’t around, making sure that Lewis didn’t get into any trouble. Not that Lewis would have done, as success at karting was everything and he appreciated just how much his father was putting into his career.

Crawley was impressed from the start of their relationship, telling James Corrigan of *The Independent*: “The first day we went to the track, we were talking and I had to check myself and remember that Lewis was just a kid and I was 25. He could hold a conversation as good as any of my friends.”

Lewis’s European forays culminated in finishing fourth in the Italian Open series, with some valuable experience gained.

“The confidence has always been there with Lewis. It’s always been part of his pysche, but mercifully it hasn’t been accompanied by arrogance. He’s as he ever was.

The 1999 season proved yet another good one as Lewis stepped up to ICA – the Intercontinental A class for faster-revving reed-valve engined karts – to race a

CRG kart for TeamMBM.com, a crack outfit run by 1982 Formula One champion Keke Rosberg. "That was quite a coincidence," said Hines, "as I'd raced against Keke in karts before he started racing cars and now here was Lewis, who I'd helped out, racing with Keke's son Nico. Also, after I ran Gary [Paffett] in the British Formula Three Championship the following year, Keke's team fielded him in the German series."

Lewis won the Italian ICA championship with team-mate Nico finishing the year as the runner-up.

Crawley was clear of their respective merits: "Whenever Lewis went on the track he would win. He was always the fastest. Against Nico, it was close, but Nico would always come second. It was a great feeling turning up knowing that we were going to win."

In addition to that Italian ICA title, Lewis was also European JICA series runner-up, with Rosberg ranked fourth overall.

The 2000 season was Lewis's crowning glory in karts as he advanced to the yet more powerful Formula A category and became the youngest ever World number one, at the age of just 15 and a half. Already European Formula A champion, after winning each of the four rounds ahead of his team-mate Rosberg and future Formula One rival Robert Kubica, and winner of the second round of the Italian Open series, Lewis was crowned World Cup champion at Motegi in Japan.

Lewis then rounded out his best ever season with the Elf Masters, an invitation race against the cream of the world's Formula Three car racers held at the Bercy indoor stadium outside Paris, beating all-comers.

Lewis beat the best of France's crop of aspiring race stars at the Elf Masters indoor event in Paris at the end of 2000.

This wonderful onboard camera shot shows Lewis at the wheel in the indoor Elf Masters event at Bercy in 2000 when he put down his marker.

AMG

“He was only 15, but he whupped all these professionals. They were amazed at what he had just done.” *Mechanic Kieran Crawley*

This provided Crawley with his abiding memory of his time with Lewis: “He was only 15, but he whupped all these professionals, all these adults. They were amazed at what he’d just done, yet all Lewis wanted to do was look at the girls. The talent was obvious, the speed was obvious and everyone knew where he’d end up. To be honest, as soon as McLaren got involved, all he had to do was work hard. It was a case of when, not if.”

Lewis’s school friends were increasingly aware of his success in karting, aware that he might actually be able to make a career out of his racing, but what probably impressed them the most was in his GCSE year when he would be dropped off in a Mercedes with his name emblazoned on its flanks, courtesy of that patronage deal with McLaren. That really meant something to those who cared not a jot for motor racing.

As reigning World Champion, Lewis raced on in Formula A in 2001, but his focus was already on stepping up to car racing as soon as he could, with plans afoot to kick off in cars that November. First, though, he stuck to his side of a bargain with his father of “no study, no karting” and moved that September to the Cambridge College of Arts and Science to study for his A-Levels. It was here that Lewis met his girlfriend, Jodia Ma.

At the end of that October, Lewis contested the final round of the World Championship on Michael Schumacher’s home track at Kerpen in Germany. As well as his usual rivals Rosberg and Vitantonio Liuzzi, the great Schumacher – already a five-time Formula One World Champion back then – took part in the event. He finished second and Lewis was a disappointed seventh after a handful of problems, but Michael had seen enough to be deeply impressed, saying: “He’s a quality driver, very strong and only 16. If he keeps this up I’m sure he will reach F1. It’s something special to see a kid of his age out on the circuit. He’s clearly got the right racing mentality.” It takes a champion to know one.

So, Lewis’s kart career was over. It had been garlanded from start to finish, his name cut onto hundreds of trophies. His name was made. Certainly, there had been jealousy from rivals at his backing from McLaren Mercedes, but Lewis had almost always made the best use of it. Now, the trick was going to be to make similar headway through single-seaters in pursuit of his F1 dreams.

TAG

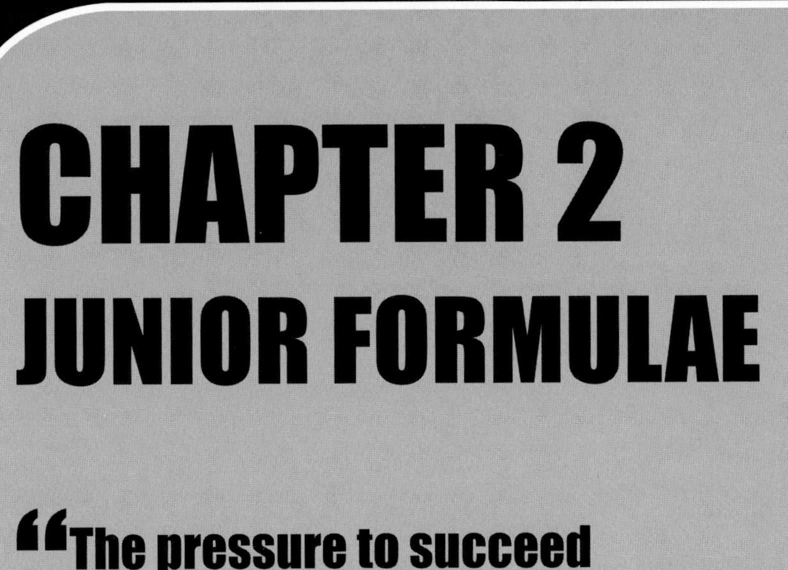

CHAPTER 2
JUNIOR FORMULAE

“The pressure to succeed came from within, from Lewis's desire to be the best.”

Formula Renault boss John Booth

JUNIOR FORMULAE

In the November of 2001, at the age of just 16½, Lewis moved on to the next stage of his passage towards his Formula One dream when he broke onto the car racing scene, arriving full of confidence to contest the two-meeting, four-race British Formula Renault Winter Series. He had been signed up by crack team Manor Motorsport, with team owner John Booth keen to give Lewis a few outings ahead of a full campaign in 2002.

This graduation didn't have an auspicious beginning when Lewis put the car into the barriers after just three laps of his first test session at the Mallory Park circuit in Leicestershire and then crashed out of his first race.

"When we tested Lewis in late 2001, he was only 16, just a kid," explained Booth. "We didn't know what to expect, but he was very mature and quiet. He had one little bump in that first test, but he was full of confidence. And we liked him, as Lewis was the kind of guy even then that people take to."

Fortunately, his raw speed was there for all to see at Rockingham when Lewis raced to fourth place in the second of the opening pair of races at the Northamptonshire circuit and then this was backed up by a fifth place finish at Donington Park to leave Lewis ranked fifth overall. Champion Rob Bell – six years older and winner of all four races – holds bragging rights to this very day, although his own single-seater hopes have since withered and left him to forge his career in sports car racing, showing just how fickle a racing career can be. It must be remembered though that Lewis was just dipping his toe in the water of the car racing pond and Manor Motorsport team manager Tony Shaw was impressed by his attacking style and his sheer confidence. All Lewis's car craft needed was a little finesse.

"Between those winter series and the start of the 2002 season, he only came up to see us once [at our Yorkshire base], for a seat-fitting," continued Booth. "But don't forget that back then he was too young to drive on the road and had to rely on his father to take him everywhere."

What was really going to mark how Lewis would affect the transition from karts to cars was his first full

» Formula Renault was Lewis's first step in car racing. He was a winner in his ninth start when he got everything right for Manor Motorsport at Thruxton in 2002.

RENAULT
MICHELIN

“We didn’t know what to expect of Lewis, but he was very mature and quiet, and full of confidence.” *John Booth*

« Lewis had targets to aim at in 2002, racers with an established Formula Renault pedigree, and he set about catching and then passing them.

season in 2002, running in the full 13-round British Formula Renault Championship, especially as he was up against former karting adversary Jamie Green and Formula Renault winter series rival Alex Lloyd. The acknowledged driver to beat, though, was Danny Watts who was racing for the rival Fortec Motorsport, and he used his greater experience to good effect to win the first two races.

Lewis started well, with a third place in the opening round at Brands Hatch before qualifying only ninth at Oulton Park next time out and then falling to 15th place by flagfall after one of the mistakes that characterised his early races. This wasn’t fitting in with Lewis’s career trajectory, but then progress was made with second place at Thruxton behind Mark McLoughlin before he tripped up at Silverstone and was placed only ninth, albeit with the race’s fastest lap to his name. This was a theme that would continue through Lewis’s ascent to the top, with a period of adjustment required before Lewis started hitting the high notes.

Success in motorsport can be achieved by finding the tiniest of advantages but then achieving that extra increment again and again and again, and so it proved as the mistakes stopped at the fifth round, at Thruxton, when Lewis boosted his confidence with victory from pole position ahead of the Fortec Motorsport duo Green and Watts at this high-speed circuit. Two more wins would follow, at Brands Hatch and Donington Park, but Watts was almost never off the podium and ended the season as champion, while Green edged Lewis back to third place overall thanks to greater consistency.

“He could have sneaked part Green at the last round to be runner-up,” said Booth. “The speed was always there, but perhaps Lewis’s biggest problem in 2002 was qualifying when he always wanted to find 2s when we fitted new tyres, rather than just 0.2s. That summed up his desire to be fastest every time he went out in the car. You could explain it to him, but as soon as the helmet went on he was on his own and would go out to blow everyone away.”

It’s said in motor racing that your best yardstick is your team-mate. This being the case,

Lewis's first full season of car racing was a clear success as he outperformed the other three Manor Motorsport drivers, with American Patrick Long, Irish racer Matt Griffin and Venezuelan hopeful Ernesto Viso ranking eighth, 11th and 20th respectively, with Long becoming a race winner only once he'd transferred to Fortec Motorsport.

Just for good measure, Manor Motorsport entered Lewis in the Formula Renault Euro Cup and Lewis rewarded the team by scoring a brace of second place finishes and a victory at Donington Park to rank fifth overall despite entering just four of the championship's nine rounds.

With his 18th birthday fast approaching, Lewis and Manor Motorsport were back for more Formula Renault in 2003, his silver over black car resplendent with TAG Heuer sponsorship. Success was required to satisfy the ambitions both of Lewis and his father, to say nothing of mentors McLaren Mercedes. Quite simply, anything less than outright championship honours would be seen as failure.

McLaren didn't apply overt pressure, though, according to Booth: "They sent two engineers up to watch over one of our rounds, but our main contact was that [Chief Executive Officer] Martin Whitmarsh would phone for a chat after every fifth round or so. It was very relaxed from McLaren actually, and the pressure came from within, from Lewis's desire to be the best."

Despite the experience Lewis gained in 2002, it took until the fifth round for Lewis to start winning, when he became the fifth different winner in this most closely-fought of training series, with Mike Conway (with Lewis finishing second), Alex Lloyd (with Lewis third), Tom Sisley and then James Rossiter (with Lewis second) having won the first four races. Fittingly, it was at the home of the British GP, Silverstone, that it all came right, with Lewis mastering wet conditions on his slick tyres to beat Sisley to the chequered flag by half a second.

Hamilton
RENAULT

TAG Heuer

“Lewis was always so fast over the first three laps of a race.”

Formula Renault rival Michael Spencer

Once that victory was in the bag, Lewis won race after race to finish the season as British champion with a tally of 10 wins. Rivals Lloyd and Rossiter could do nothing to counter this charge, even with Lewis missing the final double-header, while Lewis's team-mates Sergio Jimenez and Matthew Wilson ranked only 11th and 18th. Former kart rival Michael Spencer raced against Lewis again through 2003 and surmised that there was one particular key to Lewis's success: “He was always so fast over the first three laps of a race. You might be able to catch up again as the race went on, but he'd already done the damage by being so fast on cold tyres.”

Danny Watts and Lewis look down from the Macau Tower before the 50th Macau Grand Prix.

Lewis gathers his thoughts before heading out to try and wrap up another Formula Renault pole position. He would set 11 poles and win 10 times in 2003.

As in the autumn of 2001 when Lewis tried a few Formula Renault races at the tail-end of the season with an eye to progressing the following year, Lewis turned up with Manor Motorsport at Brands Hatch to contest the final round of the prestigious British Formula Three Championship, a series that had produced future world champions plus grand prix winners galore. He didn't come away with a win. In fact, he ended the Sunday in hospital with concussion, but Lewis had been fastest of all in wet pre-event testing and again in qualifying until he crashed and the subsequent red flag ruled out a time that would have put him an astounding fourth on the grid, so his natural speed had impressed everybody who witnessed it.

Lewis was clearly ready for the next step. Taking pole position for an international Formula Three race in Korea confirmed that he could take on the best as the season was brought to a close.

“We were new to Europe and he had no quality team-mate to work with.”

John Booth

The logical, time-honoured step would have been to enter the British Formula Three Championship in 2004, now that he knew the circuits well. With a roll call of past champions including future F1 stars Ayrton Senna, Mika Hakkinen and Rubens Barrichello, it would have been good to add his name to the list of champions. However, he, McLaren and Manor Motorsport reckoned a year spent in Europe would be more career-enhancing and so he entered the European Formula Three series. The idea was that Lewis would really get acquainted with the circuits that he would need to know when he graduated to the sport's top categories. Making matters slightly tricky was the fact that Manor Motorsport had never run a European campaign before and the fact that in Dutch driver Charles Zwolsman, Lewis didn't have a team-mate who was competitive enough to help develop the car. In a category as technical as Formula Three, where a minimal change in chassis set-up can make a massive difference to lap times, and a class where engine horsepower is limited, so drivers simply aren't able to drive around a chassis deficiency, this was something of a handicap.

To make matters harder still, Lewis had a sizeable shunt at Hockenheim in Germany in pre-season testing. So, former karting team-mate Nico Rosberg set the early-season pace by winning both races at Hockenheim before Alexandre Premat and Eric Salignon won apiece at the former home of the Portuguese GP, Estoril. The next round was at the Adria International Raceway in Italy, with Jamie Green and Salignon triumphing. Round four was around the classic Pau street course in south-west France where Green and Nicolas Lapierre shared the glory. To this point, Lewis's best result was fourth place in the first of the two races at Pau, but skill will out, and Lewis claimed victory in the fifth double-header round, held

KUMHO
TYRES
Hamilton
BOSCH
KUMHO
BOSCH
L.DUVAL

“Lewis didn’t become faster, he simply refined that speed and it all came together.”

John Booth

« Lewis learned new circuits in 2004 by contesting the Formula 3 Euroseries. Here, he congratulates runner-up Loic Duval after they came first and second in the first race at the Norisring.

on the Norisring street circuit around the Steintribune in Nuremburg. He started the first of these from pole position ahead of Lapierre and Premat, before heading home a third French driver, Loic Duval, by a couple of seconds. In the second race, Premat won from Green, with Lewis third.

Backed up with three third place finishes and a second place behind French ace Lapierre at the final race meeting at Hockenheim, Lewis ended his European Formula Three campaign fifth overall, ranked behind ASM’s duo of Green and Premat, Lapierre plus Rosberg. Team-mate Zwolsman was way off Lewis’s pace, ending up 16th overall.

“His pre-season shunt might have put Lewis on the back foot a bit,” opined Booth, “but he came good in the second half of the year. He didn’t become faster, but simply refined that speed and it all came together.”

Armed with this experience, Lewis headed east at season’s end to compete in the Formula Three invitation race at Macau, just down the Chinese coast from Hong Kong. This is, without doubt, the toughest street circuit in the world, and its victory roll reveals that it only cedes to the best, as proved by Senna, Michael Schumacher and David Coulthard having triumphed there. Lewis won the qualifying race ahead of Rosberg, Premat, the pole-starting Robert Kubica (Lewis’s team-mate for the meeting) and Green, but it all went wrong early in the main race.

Rosberg had outdragged Lewis away from the start and led onto the second lap, when he spent too much time looking in his mirrors to check whether Lewis was about to attack and simply left his braking too late into Lisboa bend and slammed into the tyrewall at this constricting right-hander. As if in sympathy, Lewis locked up as well and Premat dived past to take a lead that he wouldn’t lose for the ASM team, even after clouting a barrier midway through the race and bending his rear suspension. Rosberg was out on the spot, while Lewis had to dive up the escape road, turn around and rejoin way down the order and then make do with a chastened 14th place finish after a late-race clash with Kazuki Nakajima cost him a handful of the positions that he’d fought to regain.

Mercedes-Benz
Mobil 1
MOULIN
1960
Hamilton

Lewis relishes the rewards for an astonishing drive from 21st to victory in the 2004 Bahrain Superprix.

Lewis extended his horizons further at the end of the 2004 season with a trip to race in the Bahrain Superprix.

Straight after this, though, Lewis achieved what would be the life's ambition for most young racers: he had a run in a McLaren Formula One car at Silverstone. He was joined on this occasion by rivals Jamie Green and Alex Lloyd, both of whom had won the annual McLaren *Autosport* BRDC Award, something that Lewis wasn't free to do as he had raced at Formula Three level and was thus ineligible for this scholarship for junior British drivers. Yet, enjoy it as he did, as any driver would, to Lewis this was merely a step towards his ultimate goal. Then as it is now, this goal is to lay his name down as the greatest driver ever.

McLaren Chief Executive Officer Martin Whitmarsh was impressed: "We are all particularly delighted for Lewis that he has had this one-off opportunity. It has been a competitive season and this is a fitting reward for all the hard work that he has put in to maintain his steep learning curve." You sort of felt that this wouldn't be the last time that Lewis ever got to venture onto a circuit in a Formula One car...

As if fired up by this experience, Lewis headed to Bahrain for the season-closing Superprix for Formula Three cars. It appeared as though this was one trip too many as Lewis was caught out by the wet conditions. Yes, it rained in the desert, and his off-track excursion damaged the floor of the car, leaving Lewis 21st of the 31 starters. Fortunately, there was a qualifying race to decide the starting order for the Superprix and Lewis halved his job by climbing to 11th in this as European champion Green controlled proceedings.

What followed in the Superprix was truly remarkable as Lewis rattled past his rivals as though they weren't there in a race that looked more like a kart race. Don't forget, too, that Formula Three is famously a category in which little overtaking is done because the margin

> **"Lewis is totally confident in his abilities, so doesn't feel the need to prove himself."**
> *John Booth*

between the drivers is so close. Lewis was fourth by the time the field poured out of the first corner, with Green and Rosberg fighting over the lead and Fabio Carbone the next driver in his sights. Lewis's task was made easier when the Safety Car was deployed and he made a blinding restart to climb straight to second, although he later admitted that he had no idea how. That just left Green between Lewis and victory, but Lewis's tyres had paid the price for his furious attacks and he was unable to resist an attack from Rosberg. The Safety Car was called out again, bunching the field once more and Lewis was gifted the lead on the restart when Green hesitated slightly, surprised by the Safety Car's sudden withdrawal, and Rosberg made a move at the hairpin. With both running wide, they left the gap that Lewis needed to complete his ascent from 21st to first and give himself the perfect momentum into the close-season. This race alone proved that Lewis wasn't just quicker than his rivals but that he was a better racer and it ended his season on the highest of high notes.

That was the end of Lewis's connection with Manor Motorsport, but he is still in contact with John Booth's team. "Yes, he dropped by to see us when we were running cars in the Euro Formula Three races supporting the French GP," said Booth, "and he's just like the young guy who left us two years before. I hope that he doesn't change, but he is totally confident in his abilities, so doesn't feel the need to prove himself to others, so there's a good chance that he won't."

Lewis wanted to move up to Formula One feeder category GP2 for 2005, but long-time backers McLaren Mercedes felt he would benefit more from staying on and winning the European Formula Three crown. Lewis duly complied, and started the year as the firm favourite. The vital difference was that he had

Anthony congratulates Lewis in one of his two Formula 3 Euroseries victories at the Norisring in 2005.

Lewis's deep yellow helmet was chosen so that his father Anthony could pick him out among a pack of kart racers and it would become one of the most identifiable in car racing.

“To win at Pau, Spa and Monaco in a couple of weeks is something special.”

Mercedes Motorsport boss Norbert Haug

changed teams, leaving Manor Motorsport for ASM, the team that had helped Green to the 2004 crown, with his team-mate Premat emphasising the team's capabilities by finishing the year as runner-up. Run by Frederic Vasseur, ASM was very much the premier outfit. With a competitive team-mate in Adrian Sutil to spur him on further, Lewis hit the ground running by winning the opening race at Hockenheim and then storming to the title with 15 wins in 20 starts, usefully with victories on four circuits (Hockenheim, Spa-Francorchamps, Monaco and the Nurburgring) that host Formula One grands prix. With only a few more than half of Lewis's points tally, Sutil finished the year as runner-up ahead of Lucas di Grassi, Franck Perera and Sebastian Vettel. To dominate the championship to the extent that Lewis had was quite remarkable and this confirmed the 20-year-old as one of the hottest talents to emerge from Formula Three since Jan Magnussen blitzed the British series in 1994. Trouble was, although the talented Dane reached Formula One, his career never fulfilled his early potential and he now earns his crust racing in sports cars and touring cars, something that certainly doesn't feature in Lewis's game plan.

Highlights of the 2005 European Formula Three season for Lewis included winning around the famous Pau street circuit in the foothills of the Pyrenees in south-west France, then after taking a win at Spa following this up a couple of rounds later with victory at Monaco and beating all-comers at the Masters event at Zandvoort on the Dutch coast where the even more youthful Vettel proved to be the best of the rest.

Mercedes Motorsport boss Norbert Haug was deeply impressed: “To win at Pau, Spa and Monaco in a couple of weeks, and to win on such classic circuits in such a short space of time is something special.”

Mobil

E
L. HAMILTON
RIC

Lewis was magnificent in GP2 in 2006, winning five of the 21 rounds for ART Grand Prix and running away with the title.

PIT STOP
Puma
Intercomp

Asked whether there had been pressure from McLaren to continue to show a return on their investment, Lewis told *Autosport* magazine that the pressure was there, but it was more supportive than overt. Indeed, Lewis said that everything that McLaren wanted was what he wanted too and so the pressure was from within as well as indirectly from his Formula One mentors.

So, with the European Formula Three title freshly added to his curriculum vitae, Lewis graduated to the final step before Formula One – GP2 – in 2006 with ART Grand Prix, an outfit co-owned by Vasseur and Ferrari chief Jean Todt's son Nicolas, with Lewis taking over the seat vacated by his friend and outgoing champion Nico Rosberg.

Todt was excited by the prospect: "Lewis has proved in all of the junior formulae that he has a natural talent for driving and has displayed great professionalism. We are thrilled to be able to count on his pure speed and maturity." He was clearly right to feel such excitement, but quite how he felt knowing that Lewis would probably drive for McLaren one day against his father's Ferrari team is an unknown, although he had no choice but to pick Lewis if he wanted to have the best shot at the GP2 title.

With its identical cars, GP2 is designed to be competitive and to give the best driver, rather than the wealthiest, the opportunity to win. Even by GP2's standards, though, the category was to enjoy an unusually competitive season, studded as it was with talents such as Lewis's team-mate Premat who had ranked fourth overall in GP2 in 2005 behind current Formula One regulars Rosberg, Heikki Kovalainen and Scott Speed, plus Nelson Piquet Jr as well as Formula One refugees Timo Glock, Giorgio Pantano and Gianmaria Bruni and other hopefuls Michael Ammermuller, Adam Carroll and Nicolas Lapierre from Germany, Britain and France, respectively. With all but one of its 10 rounds taking place as the lead support for Formula One grands prix, success is doubly worth achieving as it's right under the noses of the Formula One team chiefs, not that Lewis's progress hadn't gone unnoticed to this point in his garlanded career.

Piquet Jr set the ball rolling in April by winning the opening GP2 round at Valencia for his family team ahead of Lewis, then Ammermuller won the second race of the Spanish double-header for Arden International. The next meeting at Imola was a disaster for Lewis, as he was disqualified from the first race for passing the Safety Car, and finishing only 10th in the second race, with the wins going to Bruni for Trident Racing and Lewis's 2002 Formula Renault team-mate Ernesto Viso for iSport International. However, a brace of wins at the Nurburgring put Lewis onto the attack and after losing out to team-mate Premat and Viso at Barcelona, Lewis demonstrated his affinity for Monaco by winning there. The momentum was with him and his white car with its red stripe up its nose was very much the one to beat.

As a driver who had not raced in Britain since 2003, and thus hadn't fully been picked up by the radars of occasional British race-goers, Lewis then displayed a showman's touch to win both races in front of their largest gathering for the GP2 races supporting the British GP at Silverstone. He won the first of these by passing Racing Engineering's pole-sitter Carroll into the first corner. As per the GP2 regulations, the top eight finishers start the second race in reverse order, so Lewis had some passing to do as he attempted to forge his way forward from eighth on the grid. Those who were there will long remember his three-abreast overtaking manoeuvre at Becketts when he entered the esses behind DPR Direxiv's Clivio Piccione and Piquet Jr and yet emerged at the other end of the high-speed sequence of bends in front. No other

Drivers must never forget the fans, and Lewis has always been very aware of this since once being all but ignored.

With the GP2 title in the bag, Lewis [illegible] at the end-of-season celebration at Monza. Next stop: Formula One.

ARE YOU
READY FOR
LEWIS
HAMILTON?

> **“Our objective was to win both titles, and now it is done and done well.”**
>
> *GP2 team boss Frederic Vasseur*

« These British fans are clear in their thoughts on Lewis's potential. Others, worldwide, would find out for themselves from the very start of the 2007 season.

driver would even have considered such a move. Then again, as people saw in Formula One in 2007, he is the king of overtaking, the master passer. Lewis duly went on to hunt down pole-starter and race leader Felix Porteiro. Records will list his victory as being by 10s from compatriot Carroll as Porteiro, who'd been second to the chequered flag, was thrown out for an irregularity with his Campos Racing car's steering rack. However, it was the nature of Lewis's victory rather than the final margin that will linger longest in the memories of those who saw it.

It seemed impossible that Lewis could top this, but top it he did, with a truly astonishing comeback drive in the penultimate round supporting the Turkish GP at Istanbul, fighting back from 16th place after a spin to an eventual second behind Austrian driver Andreas Zuber in the Sunday race to help ART to land its second straight teams' title, with Premat ending up third overall in the championship standings behind Piquet Jr.

By finishing third in the first of the two races at the Monza finale, behind Fisichella Motorsport International's Pantano and Piquet Jr, Lewis made the title his own. For good measure, Lewis raced to second in the closing race, pushing Pantano all the way to the chequered flag, to leave his eventual margin over Piquet Jr at 12 points.

ART boss Vasseur was more than satisfied: “Our objective at the start of the year was to win both titles and now it is done and done well.” Indeed it was.

Understandably, Lewis was also delighted at clearing his final hurdle before the big time: “It has been an amazing season, a sensational rollercoaster. There have been so many highlights and now the next target is to win the Formula One World Championship.” And he wasn't kidding.

The strangest thing about Lewis reaching the end of his ascent towards Formula One was that anyone still had any doubts over his abilities. Yet, despite his success in almost every class since his first steps in cadet karting, there are still some in the sport who largely ignore all that goes before Formula One, and these were the ones who were most shocked by what happened when he did arrive...

aigo

CHAPTER 3

THE 2007 FORMULA ONE SEASON

“I’m willing to work as hard as is needed to get to the top of my game.”

Lewis Hamilton

THE 2007 F1 SEASON

As Lewis looked ahead to 2007, with one McLaren seat thrown open by Juan Pablo Montoya's departure to race NASCAR stock cars in the USA, the crux was for whom he would race. Although he was contracted to McLaren apparently through until 2011, that didn't guarantee Lewis a race seat. Certainly, it was a relationship that had done him nothing but favours for a decade, but now was the time of reckoning and any hesitation might hold him back. However, perhaps aware that he might walk if he was offered only a test driver's role as this would interrupt his career momentum and perhaps leave him up a cul-de-sac, McLaren broke with a long-standing habit at the end of November and offered this rookie a race seat for 2007 alongside double world champion Fernando Alonso who was moving across from Renault. Some of the sport's insiders clucked at the thought of such upheaval, with not one but two new drivers meaning that there was going to be little continuity. Furthermore, there were concerns about whether it was right to put a rookie in alongside a double world champion. Rightly, Lewis had no fears about the outcome and, fortunately, nor did Ron Dennis.

"We reviewed the whole grid," Dennis told the press, "and when we looked at the drivers other than the top three [Alonso, the retiring Michael Schumacher and Ferrari-bound Raikkonen], we felt that they had pretty much reached a plateau in their careers and there was no one who really shone. In looking at Lewis both in and out of the car, he's a very polished ambassador for McLaren Mercedes and worthy of having the opportunity of showing what he can do."

Lewis, for his part, wasn't fazed by the thought of being paired with Alonso, telling *Autosport* magazine: "I feel extremely positive about it. I think the stronger the team-mate, the better. It makes you have to work even harder and I'm willing to work as hard as is needed to get to the top of my game and to beat him. If I'm given the same car, anything is possible."

With the paperwork inked, Lewis kicked off at Barcelona by putting in some serious miles for McLaren to set the ball rolling for 2007, with every lap needing to count as he gathered vital mileage.

Lewis hadn't expected to lead team-mate Fernando Alonso first time out, but he made the most of the opportunity until he had to cede to experience.

> **"I have wanted to be an Formula One driver since I started in karting and now I am."**
>
> *Lewis Hamilton*

It's not only on the test tracks that Lewis gained knowledge, as McLaren booked him in for hundreds of hours on its race simulator at its base in Woking. Not only that, but the team also employ neuroscience specialist Dr Kerry Spackman to work on his visual processing, effectively fine-tuning Lewis's already exceptionally developed racing brain so that he could match his focus and controlled aggression with the utmost consistency.

There was more testing, including one stopped short when he crashed at Valencia, more horsepower to play with, more PR duties and certainly more media exposure than ever before. So, by the time Lewis reached Melbourne for the season-opening Australian GP, he simply wanted to get out there onto the Albert Park track to do what he does best: driving. He drove well, too, ending up third fastest around this medium-speed parkland circuit and was full of excitement afterwards, saying: "I was so excited when I drove out of the garage for the first time. It was an incredible feeling as I have wanted to be an Formula One driver since I started karting and now I am and enjoying every single moment." In an instant, he became even bigger news than before and McLaren duly kept Lewis under wraps, anxious to enable him to concentrate on the task in hand.

Lewis went on to qualify impressively in fourth place, behind only Ferrari's Kimi Raikkonen, team-mate Fernando Alonso and BMW Sauber's Nick Heidfeld, but he instantly made people very aware of his uncanny racing skills on the run to the first corner. And this was despite being slow off the line and being demoted instantly by Robert Kubica. Yet, with the inside line blocked, Lewis jinked to his left and went around the outside of not only Kubica but Alonso too as they turned into the right-hander. Seasoned onlookers were amazed, their applause instant.

Then, cool as you like, Lewis raced on, being elevated to second place when Heidfeld pitted early, confirming that he had qualified his BMW Sauber with a lighter fuel load and was thus that little bit less competitive. Race leader Raikkonen also pitted before Lewis, by fully four laps, leaving Lewis to lead. After making his first ever Formula One pit stop in race conditions, he was overhauled by a recovering Alonso as Raikkonen raced on to

> **"Lewis proved worthy of the confidence we have had in him for the past 10 years."**
>
> *Norbert Haug*

victory. In taking a podium finish at his first attempt, though, Lewis made the best debut since Jacques Villeneuve raced to second place behind his Williams team-mate Damon Hill at the same Albert Park venue in 1996.

Raikkonen had won on his debut for Ferrari, but the world's press pursued Lewis afterwards, convinced that a star had been born. Well, born in the eyes of those who never look below Formula One. "I'm ecstatic," bubbled Lewis. "Today's result is more than I ever dreamed of achieving on my debut. The race was intense, and I made a few mistakes but nothing major and really enjoyed myself. It was great to lead for a few laps, but I knew it was only temporary. Fernando got past me at the second pit stop as he was able to stay out longer and I lost time behind backmarkers."

Mercedes-Benz motorsport boss Norbert Haug was full of praise: "Lewis made a perfect start to his F1 career and proved absolutely worthy of the confidence we have had in him for the past 10 years."

The three weeks until the second round of the world championship, the Malaysian GP, must have dragged as Lewis wanted to go straight back out there and do it all again. Or do even better... When it came in the sapping heat and humidity, the events at Sepang gave a clear demonstration that Lewis's Australian GP debut had been no fluke, as he braved it out around the outside of Massa at Turn 2 on lap 1, putting himself on the correct line to be ahead of the Ferrari driver as they came out of the corner. Not only did this take balls and precision, it also cemented the fact that this Formula One rookie would bow to no one. Better still

[illegible]

[illegible]

PETRONAS
PETRONAS
PETRONAS

vodafone
BRIDGESTONE
vodafone
VODAFONE McLAREN MERCEDES
VODAFONE McLAREN MERCEDES
vodafone
aigo
vodafone
aigo
vodafone
JOHNNIE WALKER
2

> **“Felipe was attacking at Turn 4 and ended up going off. It was extremely intense.”** *Lewis Hamilton*

for McLaren, it put their cars first and second and enabled Alonso to make good his escape. Massa then fought back, at Turn 4 on lap 4, but Lewis realised that he was piling into this uphill right-hander over a crest too fast and stayed out of the way then slipped back into second position on the exit. He continued to frustrate Massa, who knew that he had to get by as he was running with a lighter fuel load, until the Brazilian pushed too hard and lost several more positions as he recovered from a run across the grass out of the same corner two laps later and was never headed by him again. He later came under increasing pressure from Raikkonen in the final laps, but Lewis motored on seemingly unruffled to complete a famous one-two as Alonso took his first win for McLaren and Lewis sampled being runner-up for the first time. While the occupants of the press room were pleased for Alonso to have won, their new-found respect for Lewis was palpable.

His stunning debut in Australia made Lewis the focus of considerable media attention when he arrived for round two at Sepang.

He may have been tired, as his drinks bottle had stopped working in the Malaysian heat, but Lewis acknowledges his first second place.

“That was the toughest race of my career,” said Lewis proudly. “It was extremely exhausting defending second place. If you are on your own in the lead you have a slightly easier time than you do when you’re trying to keep your position, especially when there are two extremely quick Ferraris behind you. At one point, Felipe was attacking at Turn 4 and ended up going off the track. It was extremely intense and by the end I’d run out of drinking water, so it was tough trying to stay ahead of Kimi.”

Alonso was delighted, giving Lewis a huge embrace as they climbed out of their cars in parc ferme. “To win after coming second in Australia with my new team is like a dream come true,” he said. “To have Lewis in second place makes today’s result even better.

LF AIR
GUL
BOSS
HUGO BOSS
vodafone
FedEx
JOHNNIE WALKER
aigo
Santander
vodafone
Marlboro
PIAGGIO AERO

Team boss Dennis was equally full of praise: "There is a new spirit within the team that I believe has been witnessed by anyone who watched us. Fernando delivers a wealth of experience and racing capability, while Lewis continues to demonstrate why he has warranted the enthusiasm of all of us who have worked with him over the years."

Emphasising the contrast within the world championship calendar, the next stop just one week later was the Bahrain GP at the Sakhir circuit in the scrubby desert. This time around, humidity definitely wasn't going to be a factor in driver fatigue, although the heat was still more than 30 degrees. It was to prove a landmark race, as this was where Lewis outraced Alonso for the first time. Yes, in only his third grand prix, he'd put one over the driver adjudged to be the cream of the crop.

Chastened by his mistakes in Malaysia, Massa was the Ferrari driver to watch and raced into the lead from pole position, with Lewis chasing from the outside of the front row. Infuriatingly, Lewis's challenge dropped away on scrubbed tyres in the second stint before he closed in again in the final third of the race on his harder compound set of tyres, ending up second, just 2.2s in arrears but ahead of Raikkonen. Alonso was out of sorts and dropped from fourth to fifth behind Heidfeld to put Lewis, himself and Raikkonen sharing the championship lead.

"To have finished on the podium three times out of three is fantastic," smiled Lewis afterwards. "We have definitely closed the gap to Ferrari. I was able to keep up with Felipe in the first stint, but I had a lot of understeer in the second and wasn't able to brake as late as I would have liked. However, when I changed to hard tyres I was able to push again and, with a few more laps, I might have been able to challenge Felipe."

"Things just keep getting better and I continue living my dream."

Lewis Hamilton

"Fernando struggled with the balance of his car and we never really managed to perfect his set-up," explained Dennis. "Lewis was more comfortable with his car and had a great race."

With a break of four weeks until the Spanish GP, Lewis was champing at the bit to go racing again. And it showed in the way that he attacked on the run to the Barcelona circuit's first corner as he passed Raikkonen to climb to third. An instant later, he was second, the position gifted to him by Alonso who was too ambitious in trying to pass pole-starter Massa and ran wide into the Turn 1 gravel, much to the disappointment of the capacity crowd who had come looking for a home win.

Such was Massa's pace in race conditions that Lewis was unable to usurp him, even though he again made his first pit stop later than the Ferrari driver. Still, second place was enough to put Lewis into the championship lead, on his own. With team-mate Alonso able to recover only to third, 10s down, people were already talking of how Lewis rather than Alonso was now the McLaren team leader. As you can imagine, this wasn't going down well with the reigning world champion.

"Things just keep getting better and I continue living my dream," Lewis effused, aware that he was now out front in the world championship, leading Alonso by two points. "I was struggling to get heat into the tyres in the early stages and had oversteer, but things improved considerably a few laps into the race, although the gap to Felipe was already too big."

Wary of talk of Lewis now being seen as number one, McLaren boss Ron Dennis was balanced in his post-race comments: "Fernando's race was hampered by having damaged his deflector during his efforts to get past Massa in the first corner. It was another solid performance from Lewis."

Monaco, a fabled street circuit at which Lewis had won in Formula Three and again in GP2, was next and Lewis arrived to a barrage of questions about his relationship with Alonso, with headlines such as the one on specialist magazine *Autosport's* cover stating "Lewis is number one...but can McLaren handle it?" Asked whether the relationship had changed now that he was leading the points table, he replied: "I don't think it's changed. With the team,

By round four, the Spanish GP, Lewis was back on a circuit he knew well and gave European Formula One fans a first-hand chance to see what all the fuss was about.

movistar
RENAULT
lenovo

Last minute advice from his career mentor: Ron Dennis chats with Lewis on the grid before the Spanish GP.

Lewis is fourth on the run to the first corner at the Spanish GP, but he is about to pass Raikkonen and then Alonso will stumble to put him into second behind Massa.

the relationship grows constantly. I've been at McLaren for a long, long time, and it just gets better and better. We're very much working extremely hard together to succeed and it's going extremely well at the moment so, as you can see, it's getting better and better. With me and Fernando, the relationship is growing. We're starting to understand each other. Obviously, we've got a huge amount of respect for each other as we always have. But it's doing fine. I never thought it was a master/pupil thing to be honest. I think that as in every team, there's a little bit of rivalry, but that's only on the track. Off the track, we're friends, we can talk, we're relaxed, there's no tension there."

So, that ghost was laid to rest, but the fact that the British media was livid that Lewis came away at the end of Sunday afternoon with second place from the race throws into focus just what was expected of him, even in only the fifth race of his Formula One career. The press felt that Lewis had been fast enough to win. Perhaps he had but, as he had been running behind Alonso, McLaren urged both of their drivers to ease off, leaving factions of the media claiming that Lewis had been cheated of his first win. They even encouraged an official enquiry, accusing McLaren of fixing race orders. However, it was only common sense that McLaren didn't want its drivers to fight each other for victory, for fear of making a small mistake and hitting the barriers. With Alonso leading on merit, there was no point in asking him to pull aside and no point in leaving Lewis free to potentially put them both off with a failed passing move. The storm soon died down again when the sport's governing body, the FIA, decreed that all had been fair and just. After all, McLaren hadn't asked a quicker driver to slow down and let his team-mate through, as Ferrari did to boos in the 2002 Austrian GP.

fnac
SHOPPING
SHOPPING CENTER
METROPOLE
vodafone

> **"Fernando and Lewis responded to the team's wish of bringing both cars home safely."**
> *Ron Dennis*

Lewis toed the party line: "To finish second and run similar lap times to Fernando at Monaco makes me very happy. My start was quite good and I could run close to Fernando, but it didn't make sense to try anything crazy as our job is to ensure maximum points for the team. It's almost impossible to overtake in Monaco and your only chance is for the guy in front to make a mistake. However, Fernando is a double world champion, so I knew there would be none."

Not surprisingly, Dennis was full of praise for his drivers, especially as they had extended McLaren's lead over Ferrari to 20 points. "Fernando and Lewis responded excellently to the team's wishes of bringing both cars home safely," he said. "However, there is some disappointment because of the different strategies we needed to follow to cope with a potential deployment of the Safety Car which has happened four times in the past five years. Consequently, you have to decide in advance which one of the team's two drivers will claim the victory. Once the first round of pitstops had taken place, we reverted Lewis from a one-stop-strategy to the faster two-stop-strategy and slowed both cars to conserve the brakes. We would like to race, but this circuit requires a disciplined approach."

It was clear that it was a matter of when not if for Lewis's maiden win and it duly came in the Canadian GP at the infamous car-breaker of a track called the Circuit Gilles Villeneuve. Narrow and surrounded by concrete walls, and also completely new to Lewis, the Montreal circuit is a challenge to every driver, but Britain's new hero came out on top for his first pole position, and this was to prove important in more ways than one. Firstly, Lewis had beaten Alonso to the honour when the Spaniard slid wide at the final corner of his qualifying lap. Secondly, Lewis gained further motivation from the fact that Alonso had been lapping with a marginally lighter fuel load. Thirdly, it meant that Alonso would have to stick his neck out if he wanted to pass him. This he did, at the first corner, but it all went wrong as the Spaniard ran over the kerbs and fell back to third place behind Heidfeld, leaving Lewis free to do as he pleased. However, it's

« Lewis loves Monaco, but his hopes of victory there in F1 were kept in check when McLaren opted for a safe one-two rather than letting Lewis go for glory.

“I can’t find the words to describe what it feels like to score my first F1 win.”

Lewis Hamilton

not an understatement to write that his run to his maiden victory was far from straight-forward as it included four Safety Car periods with all of the perils of their associated restarts. Displaying maturity beyond his years, Lewis remained calm through all of these travails, his lead being slashed to nothing each time, to motor on and achieve his destiny. His father Anthony was beside himself with joy afterwards as Lewis completed an emotional slowing-down lap and then climbed jubilantly from his silver and dayglo orange racer to head for the podium to lift his first Formula One winner’s trophy and then uncork the Champagne.

At a stroke, Lewis’s success raised the bar higher as that hoped-for world title was now on his agenda, first season or not.

“I’m on another planet after this,” beamed Lewis. “I simply can’t find the words to describe what it feels like to score my first F1 win. I made an OK start, but managed to get a good exit out of the first corner and while mayhem was happening around me I was able to keep my focus. It seemed as if every time I opened up a gap the Safety Car came out and I had to start all over again. It was only a few laps from the end that I realised victory was within my grasp and I started noticing things like the fans cheering and when I crossed the finishing line it was amazing.”

Dennis was truly delighted, but kept his almost fatherly pride in check as he remembered to comment on Alonso’s troubled run to seventh place: “The frustration of Fernando receiving a stop-and-go penalty, having been forced to stop

vodafone
SAP
vodafone

Race fans aligned themselves with Lewis in a way that hadn't been seen for many a year.

Lewis required all his focus to keep cool as Alonso fought back in the battle for supremacy at McLaren.

in the pit lane when the pit lane was closed in the first Safety Car period was immense. However, this in no way should detract from a mature and disciplined drive by Lewis to claim his first win. His family should be justifiably proud of his achievement and whatever McLaren and Mercedes-Benz have contributed only compliments his talent and commitment."

This maiden victory put Lewis into a eight-point championship lead over Alonso, with Massa another seven points behind and Raikkonen six points further adrift, so it came as no surprise that Lewis's father started talking of the world title. "We can no longer say 'maybe we'll fight for the world championship'." said Anthony. "We are going for points and if we get a win that's great. We've nailed our colours to the mast now. There are no holds barred."

Next stop on the Lewis roadshow was the United States GP at the Indianapolis Motor Speedway where the American fans, including rap artist Pharrell Williams, were fully receptive to Lewis mania as America loves a winner. And Lewis instantly proved why they should.

All was not sweetness and light in the McLaren camp, though, as Alonso was feeling that he was being marginalised in a British team that was fielding a British driver. He was determined to resume control on the track, but Lewis beat him to pole when running with an identical fuel load. Lewis led away at the start, too, and kept a cool head when Alonso tried to make a move on him at over 200mph down the start/finish straight, but Lewis held firm. Then, attack rebuffed, Lewis raced on to victory, proving himself not only to be ultra-fast and fearless, but resilient too. His points lead over Alonso was now 10 points, something that would have been considered unbelievable at the beginning of the season.

Lewis was in seventh heaven: "It keeps getting better and better. I can't believe that I have won and am so incredibly grateful to the team who have worked so hard to continue the

“We were side-by-side one time, but it was all fair and square.”

Fernando Alonso

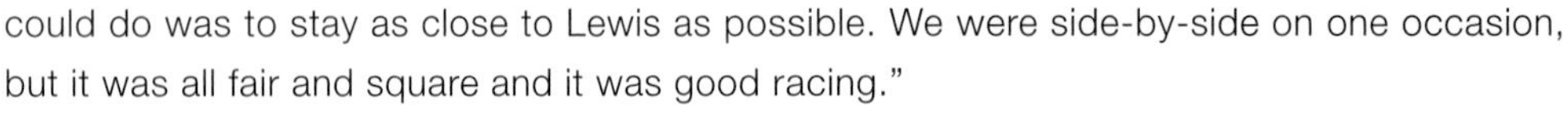

development which has seen us taking one-two here. Everything went right; start, pitstops, strategy and I'm really happy. I was under pressure all the way from Fernando and we were pushing as hard as possible. In the second stint, Fernando managed to get really close when my tyres were graining, and he had a go at the end of the straight, but I was able to keep him behind.”

Alonso was deflated afterwards, but knew that he had given it his best shot: “The race was decided after the first corner, and I didn't manage to get past. All I could do was to stay as close to Lewis as possible. We were side-by-side on one occasion, but it was all fair and square and it was good racing.”

“We were happy to let them race,” said Dennis, “but had to be mindful that our competition was not threatening our one-two finish. Their sporting behaviour both on track and especially during the podium celebrations made the team proud to have two such great drivers.”

Mercedes motorsport boss Haug had also enjoyed the spectacle: “It was a thrilling race between Lewis and Fernando. I guess we need some good nerves this year.”

Between the United States GP and the French GP, Lewis made a rare appearance in England as the star of the Goodwood Festival of Speed, where he was blown away by his rapturous reception. He was feted like a hero, was interviewed and signed autographs for the thousands, all along thinking that if this was Goodwood, just how all-encompassing would his welcome be at the British GP.

Even at Magny-Cours in the wilds of rural France, he was the flavour of the month, but this was where Ferrari was expected to fight back, at a track more suited to its longer wheelbase car, with its handful of fast, sweeping bends expected to let the F2007 show its capabilities to the full. And so it proved. However, but for a slip on his final qualifying lap, Lewis would

RBS
RBS
RBS
RBS
RBS
RBS
RBS

“I pushed hard to get past Kimi, but it didn’t work out.” *Lewis Hamilton*

still have usurped them to qualify on pole. As it was, he ended up splitting the Ferraris, but then made a terrible getaway and was immediately demoted to third by Raikkonen. Now this was a problem, as Lewis was starting with a lighter fuel. Thus, for each lap that he spent hemmed in behind the Finn, not only could Massa pull away in the lead, but his advantage was being wasted. Lewis pushed and prodded, but could do nothing to elevate his position and bad almost turned to worse when McLaren elected to short-fuel him at his second pit stop, putting him on to a three-stop run, and Lewis was passed by Kubica’s BMW Sauber as he rejoined. The Pole still had a stop to make, but Lewis couldn’t afford to be delayed for a moment and promptly pulled off one of the moves of the season when he outbraked him into the Adelaide hairpin. It was a blinder of a move and paid off as the potential loss of time was eliminated and he was duly able to race on to that third place to extend his championship lead to 14 points over Alonso who had had to start 10th after a gearbox failure and then fought like a wild man to work his way through the midfield, ending up seventh.

“I didn’t have the best start and I don’t know exactly what the reason was,” said a still upbeat Lewis afterwards. “My car was very good in the opening stage of the race, and I pushed hard to get past Kimi, but unfortunately it didn’t work out, so we opted for a three-stop strategy.”

Dennis explained the change of tactics: “We had the option of switching between a two or three-stop strategy for Lewis, and we opted for the latter to ensure that he had minimal traffic and maintained his strong and safe third position.”

Asked post-race about the thrill of heading to his home race with a 14-point lead, Lewis replied: “I keep

Lewis and Felipe Massa get on well, both enjoying usurping their more established team-mates Alonso and Raikkonen.

Felipe Massa lines up on pole position at Magny-Cours, but Lewis, in second grid position, would soon lose ground.

Mercedes-Benz
vodafone
BOSS
aigo
vodafone
POTENZA
BRIDGESTONE

Lewismania doubled the size of the crowd for the practice days at the British GP, then filled it to capacity on race day, helped by Lewis bagging a dramatic pole.

> **"Going to my first British GP leading the championship is one of the greatest feelings."**
>
> *Lewis Hamilton*

saying that I didn't even expect to finish on the podium in my first race let alone the first eight races of the season, so I am very happy with the job that I have done and the job that the team have done and I think that going into my first British GP with the team that I have always wanted to drive for and leading the world championship is one of the greatest feelings that a driver can have."

The weather had been wet, wet, wet in Britain for the month that led up to the British GP. The fields surrounding Silverstone were saturated. No more rain could be contained and there was fear that the campsites would turn into quagmires. Yet, lo, the skies started brightening on the Friday, the first day of the meeting. Lewis was fast, too, but the Ferraris were faster. A record crowd of 42,000 felt confident however sure that Ferrari wouldn't waltz away as they had at Magny-Cours. By Saturday, though, Lewis had charmed double that number to attend (this a record for a British GP Saturday crowd). He even laid on blazing sunshine and, showing that miracles were his stock-in trade, he saved his best shot until last in qualifying to snatch pole at the death. Father Anthony jigged in the pit lane, and the packed grandstands erupted. They were all living the dream, and Lewis said later that he'd been disappointed with the lap, feeling it beneath the level he desired, showing just how high his sights are set. For the fans, though, it looked just fine, sending them back to their fast-drying campsites in high spirits. The only dark cloud on the horizon was the fast escalating espionage story centred on McLaren chief designer Mike Coughlan.

Race day wasn't as kind and, after a mistake at his first pit stop, when Lewis attempted to leave before the fuel hose had been disengaged, the lead was taken by Alonso. Then, after the second round of stops, it was Ferrari's Raikkonen in control as Lewis dropped ever further back in third. It was disappointing for a crowd that had been led to believe that Lewis could walk on water and would sweep all before him on his homecoming. Yet, when the hub-bub subsided, McLaren were left to reflect on their decision a few weeks earlier to keep Lewis away from the pre-British GP tests at Silverstone to shield him from publicity. Perhaps those extra laps might have made all the difference.

“The race would have been harder without the fans’ support.” *Lewis Hamilton*

“I got a good start and tried to pull out a gap, but Kimi was extremely quick,” explained Lewis. “Unfortunately, I made a mistake in the pit stop, which cost me a few seconds. I tried to drive around balance issues and, although I was more consistent towards the end, the team chose to save the engine for the Nurburgring. Starting with the harder tyre was not the best way to go as the softer tyre was clearly faster. The fans have been tremendous, and the race would have been harder without their support.” Lewis then vowed to “dig deeper” to attempt to stay in the lead of the title race, blaming his lack of knowledge on set-up causing him to go down the wrong path.

Dennis was sanguine about being beaten by Ferrari for the second race in a row: “Fernando did a tremendous job, making every effort to turn our short-fuel middle stint into a win. Ultimately, he and Lewis were asked to turn their engines down to ensure that we had the best ability to attack again in Germany.”

The European GP at the Nurburgring was next, and Lewis needed to re-establish himself after Raikkonen’s double for Ferrari at Magny-Cours then Silverstone. Fortunately, the circuit’s layout, with more medium-speed twists and turns and fewer, high-speed turns would be better to suited to the McLaren. Add to that the fact that Lewis had dominated the GP2 races there in 2006 and you can understand why his mood was more positive.

He was still able to top the timesheets in the first of Friday’s practice sessions and be faster than all but Raikkonen in the afternoon. He was second behind the Finn again on the Saturday morning, but the images beamed around the world on the Saturday afternoon caused Lewis fans to gasp, for there was their hero mounting the kerbs early in final qualifiying, skipping across a gravel bed and slamming into the tyre wall at 150mph. It was a while until the rescue crew released him from the cockpit. By then, the replays had shown that the accident wasn’t Lewis’ fault, as his right front wheel had come loose and its tyre was cut, deflating suddenly. Dennis confirmed that this was down to a fault with the wheelgun. He remained clearly worried, despite a winded Lewis having shown a thumbs-up as he was stretchered into the ambulance, as he had had no further news. It later became clear that Lewis was

This is what happens when you have a tyre deflate at 150mph, going into a corner, as Lewis discovered in the final qualifying session at the Nurburgring.

Mobil
2
SAP

« Victory in Hungary was doubly valuable as it not only helped Lewis bounce back after the Nurburgring, but came after a weekend of considerable acrimony.

unhurt, just shaken. So, providing he was cleared to race, his title aspirations were still on, albeit with his starting position being 10th rather than the first two rows he'd surely have achieved had he completed qualifying.

It was dry as Raikkonen accelerated away from pole, but Lewis was the one on the move, having passed four cars by the first corner. Out of Turn 2, he was up to fourth after the BMWs tangled, but he'd clipped one when it spun and picked up a puncture. Rain hit as he had a slow drive back to the pits, during which the downpour had transformed Turn 1 into a lake and, even on rain tyres, he joined car after car that had aquaplaned off there. The difference was, Lewis kept his engine going and was craned out, losing a lap, but able to take the restart.

Lewis drove like a demon in pursuit of any points that he might recover. With rain making a second visit in the final few laps, he missed out on scoring by 1.5s, having passed Giancarlo Fisichella a lap from home and closed in on Heikki Kovalainen. At least McLaren ended up with a winner, with Alonso barging his way past Massa five laps from home, but this meant that Lewis's points lead had all but evaporated, plunging to just two.

What Lewis really needed after the European GP was to regain his momentum. What McLaren really needed was to put the spying allegations behind them and get back to racing first and foremost at the Hungarian GP.

Lewis achieved the former but neither escaped the world of intrigue after a bizarre third qualifying session in which Lewis was delayed in the pits by Alonso to the extent that he didn't have enough time to get back onto the track to complete his final flying lap before the chequered flag fell at the end of the session, offering him no opportunity to regain pole after his team-mate snatched it from him. The incident was so peculiar and the explanations so confusing that the stewards took almost until midnight to decide on their response: they charged Alonso with impeding an opponent and moved him back from first to sixth.

The stewards' ruling elevated Lewis to pole and moved him from the dirty side of the grid.

A good start would be imperative, particularly on a circuit where overtaking is so hard to do. Heidfeld lined his BMW Sauber across at him from the outside of the front row, but the usually fast-starting German was not Lewis's equal, and he also lost out to Raikkonen's Ferrari.

And so started a dogfight that would last until the chequered flag.

There were occasions when Raikkonen was right on his tail, with Lewis troubled in his second stint by a steering wheel that was angled to the right, but he took the gap out from 1s to 4.4s thanks to a handful of quick laps when he stayed out four laps longer before making his final pit stop. But then Raikkonen banged in a series of laps that were fully 1s faster than Lewis and was back on his tail. Now was the time for Lewis to dig deep, to keep his cool and to refrain from the merest of slips, something that wasn't always easy when negotiating traffic, with Sato giving him a particular scare when he emerged from the pits into his path at Turn 1.

Lewis was pumped up, his determination to win greater than ever after the perceived lack of fairness in qualifying and he tied it all up for his third win from 11 starts.

With Alonso delayed by Ralf Schumacher in the early laps and just failing to find a way by Heidfeld for third, Lewis stretched his points advantage from two points to seven.

After the trials and tribulations of Hungary and a break of two weekends, it was back into action for Lewis and the gang at the Turkish GP at the end of August. The media, given so much opportunity to fan the flames at the Hungaroring, were keen to follow up on the antagonism between Lewis and Fernando, but after a team meeting to clear the air on the Thursday neither driver offered them much succour.

On the track, though, there was a more immediate enemy: Ferrari. Indeed, McLaren had feared that the Italian team would have the upper hand around the fast, open curves of the Istanbul circuit and so it proved as Massa claimed pole. It had been incredibly close, though, with Lewis lapping just 0.044s slower to line up second ahead of Raikkonen and Alonso. The race would prove that he had been carrying an extra lap of fuel too, so a different gamble could have seen him starting from pole.

vodafone
DIAGEO
Mobil 1
BOSS

Alonso leads Lewis in a McLaren one-two ahead of the Ferraris in the early laps of the Italian GP on a weekend when F1 needed sport to come to the fore.

This would have had an extra advantage in that not only would it have given Lewis track position, but also the clean side of the circuit from which to start. As it proved, Raikkonen shot past Lewis before Turn 1 and there was nothing that he could do to overturn the deficit in those two laps between Massa pitting from the lead and Lewis coming in for his first stop.

Put simply, the Ferraris had the legs in Turkey, but Lewis's hopes of being best of the rest went awry when his right front tyre delaminated as he powered out of Turn 8 then blew at Turn 9 on lap 43, three laps before his second pit stop was scheduled. At least Lewis was halfway around the lap, so he was able to limp back to the pits, rubber flailing, and continue with fresh rubber. Had he had the tyre fail at the start of the lap, he might have failed to make it back. As it was, he rejoined in fifth, behind Alonso and Heidfeld, a position that he was able to hold to the end to collect four points, so it was a hiccup rather than a disaster. Had he lost control when the tyre blew, that margin over Fernando would have been down to just one.

By the time of the Italian GP a fortnight later, intra-team troubles had quietened down, but the spectre of the FIA's World Motor Sport Council making judgment on spying charges against the team on the Thursday after the race left McLaren less than chirpy. As if in response, the team collected the only result that would suit them: they beat Ferrari on home ground. This powerplay against arch-rivals Ferrari began with a McLaren lock-out of the front row, with Fernando landing pole by 0.037s from Lewis. Knowing that he was fuelled a couple of laps shorter than Fernando, Lewis needed to get in front at the start if he was to stop his team-mate from cutting into his points advantage. But this is not what happened. Unusually, Lewis made his bid for the lead despite having been outdragged on the run to the first corner by Massa, with Raikkonen also pressing him. But his demon outbraking manoeuvre was then compromised, as he explains: "I didn't get the best getaway and Felipe managed to shoot past me. I outbraked both him and Fernando into Turn 1, and I almost thought I was going to get past, but then Felipe clipped me and sent me over the second part of the chicane."

Before the lap was out, though, the safety car had been deployed as David Coulthard had crashed his Red Bull at Curva Grande after its suspension failed following contact at the first

"Initially I thought 'oh thanks', but I guess these things happen when you fight for the World Championship."

Lewis Hamilton

chicane with Giancarlo Fisichella's Renault. He was OK and Lewis was thus given a second chance to try and wrest the lead from Fernando. It didn't work and Lewis's team-mate eased clear from there.

Any further challenge from Massa faded when he retired with damper failure and so it was left to Raikkonen to try and topple the McLarens. The tactic that might have helped him was to run a one-stop strategy to their two, something that had become apparent as a possibility when he qualified only fifth, 1.186s off the pace. He wasn't as fast as they were, but he was saving the 22s or so needed for that second pit stop and so both Fernando and Lewis had to charge. Indeed, having suffered from a flat-spotted front tyre, Lewis fell to third behind the Finn after his second stop and only got his place back with a stunning move three laps later, before his fresh tyres had gone off.

This came at the first chicane and was shockingly bold. Lewis raced on to second, but Fernando's win cut his advantage to just three points.

"I was suffering vibrations on my tyres in the second stint," Lewis explained, "so I opted to pit earlier to play it safe. With Kimi on a one-stop strategy, it was key to optimise my second stop. Unfortunately I came out behind him, but I knew I was faster on the new tyres, if only for a couple of laps, and so I just took the opportunity when I caught him up. It was really important for me to get that place back, not only for my position in the championship, but also for all the team. We had the one-two in qualifying yesterday, and to maintain this in the race was the icing on the cake."

Team boss Dennis was delighted: "To have McLaren's first one-two at Monza is really special. The entire team has done a fantastic job both on and off track in difficult circumstances, and our dominance this weekend is a just reward for all their efforts. Fernando and Lewis put in excellent performances and Lewis's overtaking manoeuvre to reclaim second showed his determination."

There was only a week between the Italian GP and Formula One's return to Spa-Francorchamps, but it was a momentous one, with McLaren having all of its points towards the constructors' championship erased by the sport's governing body, the FIA, turning its 23-

Lewis attends the FIA World Council meeting in Paris to offer support and to discover if he would be stripped of his drivers' points.

23-point lead over Ferrari into a 57-point lead for Ferrari over BMW Sauber. That the team was also fined $100m left all of motor racing, and sport in general, reeling. If there was a consolation, it was that FIA President Max Mosley had failed in his wish that both Lewis and Fernando – first and second in the drivers' championship – be stripped of their points as well. So it was hardly surprising that McLaren felt embattled as they went about their business on their arrival in Belgium.

Pulling off another one-two to match that achieved at Monza would have been some sort of panacea, but Spa-Francorchamps was always going to suit Ferrari's F2007 rather than the MP4-22. And so it proved as Raikkonen claimed pole position, with Massa second, Fernando third and Lewis fourth.

What fans will remember of the race, aside from Ferrari's dominance of proceedings and the fact that Raikkonen made it three wins in a row at the magnificent Belgian circuit, is what happened at the first corner on the opening lap, for this is where Fernando and Lewis got close enough to get to know each other even better than they did already, with Fernando forcing Lewis wide out of the La Source hairpin.

What happened was that Fernando had got bunched by Massa's out-of-position Ferrari and Fernando had to back off to avoid hitting him. But he raised eyebrows when he swung all the way to the outside kerb as they exited the corner, pushing Lewis onto the run-off area. Lewis was less than happy, saying: "I got a good start and thought I had a chance to get past at the first corner, but I had to run wide as Fernando kept to the inside line. Initially I thought 'oh thanks', but I guess these things happen when you fight for the World Championship."

Fernando had his view of events. "At the start," he said, "I was sticking to the inside line as long as possible. Unfortunately, Lewis ran wide, as there was no space left and I knew there was plenty of run-off area. I knew that my car in the first stint would be a bit faster as

Fed

> “When you have two great drivers like Fernando and Lewis fighting for the World Championship, you have to expect manoeuvres like we saw today.”
>
> *Ron Dennis*

I was stopping a lap earlier than Lewis, so it was very important to be in front.”

This view was supported from the sidelines, team boss Ron Dennis who reckoned that it had been a fair, racing incident, which was most magnanimous considering that he revealed at Spa that he and Fernando hadn't been on speaking terms since the Hungarian GP. Dennis said: “When you have two great drivers like Fernando and Lewis fighting for the World Championship, you have to expect manoeuvres like we saw today at the start, which are a result of both being extremely competitive.”

Lewis wasn't about to give up though, and was alongside as they accelerated down the hill towards Eau Rouge, once one of Formula One's most fearsome corners. Fortunately for both, it's now less so, but Lewis still braved it out side-by-side through the left-hand part before opting for safety over possible glory, slotting back into Fernando's wake.

As early as the first lap, it was clear that Ferrari's straightline speed was simply too much for the McLarens and so they pulled away. Massa was unable to match Raikkonen and so the order at the front remained unchanged. By flagfall, Fernando was 10s behind second-placed Massa, with Lewis a further 9s adrift.

With Lewis finishing only fourth, his lead was cut to just two points over Fernando, while Raikkonen's victory moved him to within 13 points of the top of the table, so the battle was really hotting up with three rounds remaining.

When people look back over 2007, Lewis's Japanese GP will shine out. For it was on the sideslopes of Japan's Mount Fuji, with the war of words with Alonso increasing by the minute, that Lewis displayed a James Bond-like cool to win a race run in the most extreme conditions for a generation.

« Lewis's fourth-place finish in the Belgian Grand Prix meant that his Championship lead would be reduced to just two points.

In truth, many felt that Fuji was where Alonso's growing momentum would move him past Lewis. There had been but two points between them, but Lewis was the man in qualifying. Not by a lot, 0.07s, but the benefit was multiplied when the track was shrouded in fog on race day and

Hamilton's Japanese Grand Prix triumph in atrocious conditions meant that he was now in pole position to win the Drivers' Championship.

straked with rain. There were echoes of 1976 when James Hunt claimed his world title here, but this time the race was started behind the safety car. It pulled in after 19 laps. The risk of aquaplaning lurked at every turn. Lewis kept his focus, but Heidfeld tipped Button into a spin and Wurz was put out of the race by Massa as those behind concertinaed.

The Ferraris were soon out of the reckoning, having not started on extreme wets, so Lewis had only Alonso as a rival. It all could have gone wrong on lap 34 when Kubica clattered into Lewis. "I didn't see him coming," said Lewis, "so the impact caught me by surprise, and I spun." This dropped Lewis behind Kovalainen, but he was back in the lead five laps later when the Finn pitted, and the pressure eased on lap 43 when Alonso crashed out of the race, leaving Lewis in a considerably stronger championship position.

So, after two hours of slithering about, in which Lewis never put a foot wrong, his points advantage over Alonso stretched to 12, with Raikkonen 17 behind, his outside chance continuing thanks to scrabbling his way back to third behind Kovalainen after Vettel clattered Webber out of second place.

Some said the title was as good as settled, but Lewis wasn't celebrating yet: "This was an important win, but I don't want to think too much about it and will focus hard on the Chinese GP." Yet, all were in agreement with Ron Dennis when he described Lewis's performance as "masterful."

The title was there for the taking. Lewis's 12-point lead offered the facility to either land the title in Shanghai with a minimum of second place or to run around to third or fourth and then finish the job off with a gentle drive in Brazil.

After practice, Lewis appeared to be third or fourth fastest. Yet, after qualifying, Lewis had grabbed pole.

Under leaden skies, Lewis made a perfect start. Raikkonen was safe in second, but Alonso passed Massa as they exited Turn 2 before a slow exit from Turn 3 enabled Massa to regain third at the first hairpin. Lewis was 0.7s clear at the end of lap 1 and going away. On the pitwall, all eyes were on the sky as rain blew in.

“Don’t worry, there’s a race to go so I can still do it.”

Lewis Hamilton

Lewis was the first to pit, on lap 15 from an 8.6s lead, but only for fuel as he kept on his intermediates. He re-emerged in fourth ahead of David Coulthard. The key would be how much longer Raikkonen would run and he set a series of fastest laps before stopping on lap 19. The gap came down to 4s.

What followed was perplexing as Raikkonen made his first attack on lap 28, Lewis fought to hold him off. Why? All he needed was eight points and this was with Alonso winning, not Raikkonen.

Raikkonen took the lead on lap 29 when Lewis slid wide. At this point, dry tyres were the ones to have as Alex Wurz had had them fitted and was lapping fastest. It was up to the teams to read the changing conditions, and McLaren were to leave him out too long on tyres that were shot, the canvas visible on the left rear tyre.

When Lewis peeled into the pits on lap 31, he ran wide and his car became stuck in a gravel trap. His only hope was that the win wouldn’t go to closest rival Alonso who had closed onto his tail.

Lewis stormed off, helmet on to avoid speaking to the media. A while later, he talked to the press in a comfortingly upbeat manner. Showing positive mind management, Lewis said: “Don’t worry, there’s a race to go so I can still do it.”

In Brazil, the message was still beamed out that everything was going to be alright. Then the rain fell and the Ferraris were faster... Yet Lewis learned the Interlagos circuit in a flash and was fastest when it dried.

Lewis had to focus on qualifying, Massa went top, but Lewis slotted in a stunning middle section on his final flier and was ahead going into the long final corner. He just missed pole, but his lap was good enough for second on the grid and, perhaps most importantly, Alonso would start two places further back, behind Raikkonen. “I’m where I need to be,” Lewis grinned. That just left the race...

» A dejected Hamilton walks away from his McLaren following his retirement on lap 31 of the Chinese Grand Prix. This meant that the Championship would go to the last race of the season.

vodafone
JOHNNIE WALKER
SAP
Mobil 1
BOSS
vodafone
SAP
"MM" MUTUA MADRILEÑA
vodafone
sparco

Red Bull
vodafone
DENSO
TOYOTA
FLY
KINGFISHER

« A dejected Lewis Hamilton is consoled by fellow British driver David Coulthard following his seventh place in Brazil, which was not enough to clinch the 2007 Drivers' Championship.

The fact that Hamilton lost a place to Raikkonen at the start wasn't a disaster, but the Finn then tripped over Massa out of the first corner and had to lift off. Lewis did too to avoid him and this enabled Alonso to have a run into turn 3 and get past. Lewis then lost his cool at the next corner in his desire to get back into third, locked up and ran off the track. He rejoined eighth and suddenly there was a mountain to climb.

On lap 8, his McLaren slowed and 30s were lost before it got up to speed again as a gear-shifting problem was fixed with advice radioed from engineer Phil Prew. Eighth had become 18th. The title was no longer Lewis's to lose but Lewis's to win back.

Lewis had to start overtaking and fast. This he did, even passing four cars on one lap. Mark Webber retiring handed him another place, so Lewis was up to 10th when he pitted. He then pressed like mad, with a heart-in-mouth moment when he dived inside Barrichello's Honda.

Alonso was unable to keep with the Ferraris and was being troubled by Kubica. Then commentators noticed that Lewis's second stop appeared quick and suggested he might have been short-fuelled.

Sadly, having risen to eighth by lap 56, Lewis did have to pit for a third time scuppering any chance he might have had of catching Heidfeld and working his way towards the fifth place that he would need now that Raikkonen had moved to the front after his second stop. He got back one place when Trulli pitted, but that was it, barring disasters for those ahead. Certainly, Kubica and Rosberg's battling might have led to both falling off and gifting two places to Lewis. The two places that he needed. But it never happened and seventh was all he could manage, leaving the tally at 110 points for Raikkonen and 109 each for Lewis and Alonso.

There was disappointment but also pride, and the final words on a debut F1 season that so nearly produced the first world title for a rookie ought to go to Lewis: "I am pretty disappointed, having led for so much of the season and then not to win the championship. However, I have to put the result into perspective: this is only my first year in F1 and overall it has been phenomenal. I am still very young and have plenty more years in me to achieve my dream."

LEWIS: IN CONCLUSION

Michael Schumacher shocked the establishment when he broke onto the Formula One scene at Spa-Francorchamps in 1991. It took a further year, precisely, before he became a winner and until the end of his third full season to become world champion, but when he retired at the end of 2006, he did so as a seven-time world title winner. Lewis almost pulled it off at his first attempt, failing by just one point after clipping the final hurdle. It would take a brave gambler, though, to bet against him going one better in 2008.

Endless fanfares were sounded as Lewis ascended motor racing's ladder to Formula One. Yet still he astounded on his debut in Melbourne. Not only did Lewis claim a podium first time out, but he combined the audacity not only to overtake into the opening corner, around the outside, but then to lead his established team-mate, the reigning world champion, Fernando Alonso. Quite simply, people were bowled over.

The impact that Lewis made in his first season of Formula One was incredible. He was young, fresh, sassy, downright fast and a supreme racer. He was everything that the sport needed to power itself to the next level, to shake off the torpor with which it had been cloaked since the days at the start of the decade when Schumacher dominated all.

On top of this, Lewis also struck onlookers as being freakishly normal, almost the boy next door in his approach to life and thus opened Formula One up to those who had previously thought it elitist. He had made it all so believable. Well, all of it apart from the politics in which Formula One tends to wallow.

Most importantly, Formula One was back on the map, back in people's minds and even on the front pages of newspapers. Rivals may have become tired of the way that practically every story about Formula One related to Lewis in some way or other, but they were wise enough to realise that they all benefitted from the upsurge of interest, as new sponsors were looking at the grand prix world as never before.

The level of interest in Lewis was a phenomenon. If you think that the adulation came from Britain alone, think again. Lewis's youth, his background, his vim and his vigour make him universal, a face fit to adorn billboards in every city in every country in the world. Small wonder

Such a determined character as Lewis Hamilton will no doubt be disappointed that he did not clinch this year's championship, however, he is already strongly tipped to realise his dream next season.

that there is already talk that he might pocket £1 billion over his career...

Excited and empowered by that, a whole new wave of wannabes are clamouring to go racing. As Lewis has opened the door for more and more children from a far more universal spectrum of society than before to see if they can cut it in karting.

Lewis has also helped the best of those already fighting their way through the junior ranks of car racing, as all the top teams are now looking to find "the next Lewis" and signing up the most promising of these drivers on multi-year contracts, something that in many cases is saving their careers from faltering due to a lack of money, an affliction that has hit so many before them.

When it comes to overtaking, too, Lewis is the man. Who can forget, after all, his brilliant first corner antics in Australia, his I-shall-not-be-beaten resistance of Massa in Malaysia, his incisive dive past Robert Kubica in France or his no holds barred pass of Kimi Raikkonen in Italy? Enough said.

If Lewis's speed and outstanding race craft is his trademark, what really sets him apart from other rookies is his ability to stay calm when the pressure ramps up. Strong focus is a clear attribute. Sure, he has been racing since childhood and has landed in Formula One with one of the two most competitive teams, but what has made it all but too impossible to believe that he is a Formula One rookie has been the way that he has driven without error when all around him were fumbling. Take the Canadian GP, which he won despite seemingly constant periods of safety car deployment breaking the natural flow of the race. His focus

“I will go into next season with my head held high and know we will come back even stronger.” *Lewis Hamilton*

» The impact of Lewis Hamilton's first Formula One season has been incredible and has revitalised the public's appetite for the sport.

never wavered and he walked away with that famous first victory. That Lewis managed to cruise to victory at the Japanese GP, too, when conditions were horrific and fellow driver Alexander Wurz described the lack of visibility like “running through your house with your eyes closed,” also put you in mind of Schumacher at his pomp. There was that costly slip-up when he dropped his car into the gravel bed at the pit entrance in Shanghai, but the team took most of the blame for that for leaving him out too long on tyres that were all but worn through. Perhaps, just perhaps, Lewis's calm failed him when the pressure was its greatest in the Brazilian finale, as he pushed harder than he might to make up for losing two places through the first three corners and then falling off in his quest to regain one of them. This wasn't what ultimately cost him the title – that was the 30s lost by his gearbox glitch – but it's the sort of error that he will have to eliminate to become champion, as he almost assuredly will, whether in 2008 or further into the future.

Time and again, drivers who have possessed great, natural speed have burned brightly, but flickered like a candle in the wind once in Formula One. The reasons for this are manifold, but what Lewis has shown is that you need to possess the whole range of capabilities. These have to include the ability to drive fast, of course, but also the ability to race wheel-to-wheel and to overtake. Plus the ability to understand the technical side of the sport and to be able to offer valid feedback to your engineers. The ability to get on with your team is vital too, as you never know when a useful development part might need someone to race it. Shining under the media spotlight is also crucial, especially if a driver wants to keep media interest the right side of intrusion, to be allowed to keep as normal a life as possible. Finally, the ability to work with sponsors completes the package, to say nothing of adding to that driver's bank balance. So, you can understand why so many have failed to reach the top, often falling down in just one of these areas or, sadly, just by being with the wrong team at the wrong time.

The sport is fickle, but the likes of Michael and Lewis are armed with the skills to counter that. And that's why Lewis is where he is now.

What a year, what a driver, what a future.

JOHNNIE WALKER
Mobil
1

FedEx
BOSS

CHAPTER 4

IN PRAISE OF LEWIS

"He is the best driver to hit F1 in 60 years, and the best prepared too."

Sir Stirling Moss

IN PRAISE OF LEWIS

The accolades have been rolling in since Lewis first raced in karts, but they turned into a torrent when he made his instant splash in Formula One. Even his team-mate had nice things to say about him.

Indeed, Fernando Alonso was asked after the Spanish GP whether Lewis had become a different opponent:

> **"After one or two races, we saw Lewis become a championship contender. I look at him the same way I look at Kimi or Felipe, opponents for the championship. I have to beat them all if I want to become champion, but he is the one who worries me least because he is my team-mate and we are here to help each other."**

Another driver from the McLaren camp, test driver Pedro de La Rosa also shared his thoughts:

> **"Fernando's arrival at the team has brought great leadership. Lewis brings youth and is always pushing. Lewis has actually been with the team for a long time. We've been working together for a few years, so I feel like Fernando is newer to the team than Lewis is, but they both bring very good things."**

The perspective of age and distance often produces the greatest clarity and *The Daily Telegraph* extracted some wonderful sound bites from Sir Stirling Moss, the greatest driver never to have been crowned world champion.

> **"My all-time great was [Juan Manuel] Fangio," the 78-year-old told Martin Smith, "and one of the great things about Fangio, apart from his enormous ability, was the sort of man he was. Lewis is the same sort of person: he is**

At the start of the 2007 campaign, Lewis was happy to play the role of 'new boy' alongside Alonso, but the plaudits were soon matched by winning results.

very humble, tremendously fast and has great concentration." Moss added: "Until Lewis arrived, Alonso was the best and I feel sorry for him. After all, he'd probably never heard of the guy until earlier in the year, and suddenly here's a man as great as Fangio and [Tazio] Nuvolari, beating him."

At the Goodwood Festival of Speed in July, Moss added:

"Lewis is the best thing I've ever seen, the best driver to hit F1 in 60 years, and the best prepared too."

Ex-F1 racer turned TV pundit Mark Blundell:

"Lewis played the rookie card beautifully, while all along believing he was as good if not better than all the guys out there."

"MM"
JOHNNIE
SAP
Mobil
1
BOSS
vodafone

« Having competitive machinery is one thing, but it's the way that Lewis has made the most of it that has impressed the likes of former world champion Nigel Mansell.

Team chief Sir Frank Williams added his ready wit, saying:

> **"After we'd got rid of Michael [Schumacher], I thought 'now we've got a chance again', but then another superhuman turns up."**

The most recent British world champion, Damon Hill who did the trick in 1996, told *Autosport* magazine:

> **"I've never seen a rookie as good as Lewis. Nothing more could be asked of him, really. He's coped with everything he's faced: he's been superb.The closest thing that you can compare Lewis to is a child prodigy musician, somebody picked up and celebrated at a very young age."**

Nigel Mansell, world champion in 1992, told *Autosport* that he thought Lewis has been "absolutely outstanding and brilliant," going on to say:

> **"The timing has also been perfect for him, as for any driver to start his career with a team that's just returned to the front of the grid is fantastic. Barring accidents and misfortune, he has got all the credentials to be a world champion."**

Three-time F1 World Champion, Sir Jackie Stewart:

> **"Lewis doesn't have full experience yet. In three years' time, he is not going to know himself. He is going to be fully rounded and China wouldn't happen in three years' time."**

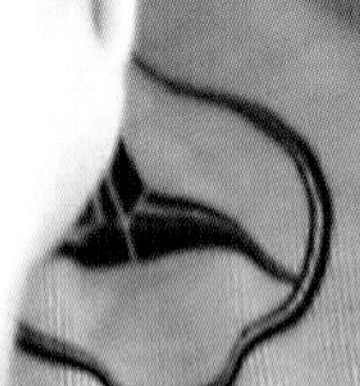

CHAPTER 5
RECORDS & STATISTICS

“Never give up, not under any circumstances. When the going gets tough, just keep on pushing.”

Lewis Hamilton

RECORDS & STATISTICS

Lewis's record as he rose through the ranks from cadet kart racer to grand prix winner has been astonishing. His career stats show how he claimed 16 titles and collected more than 300 trophies, but it hasn't been victory every time out, as there have been periods of learning and adjustment as he graduated to more advanced categories before he put it all together, bested his rivals and was crowned champion again.

1993 CADET KARTS

1994 CADET KARTS

1995 CADET KARTS
- British champion
- STP Cadet champion

1996 CADET KARTS
- McLaren Mercedes Champions of the Future champion
- Sky TV Kart Masters champion
- Five Nations champion

1997 JUNIOR YAMAHA KARTS
- McLaren Mercedes Champions of the Future champion
- British champion

1998 JICA (Junior Intercontinental A) KARTS
- McLaren Mercedes Champions of the Future runner-up
- Italian Open series, fourth

1999 JICA & ICA (Intercontinental A) KARTS
- Italian Industrials ICA champion
- European JICA runner-up
- Italian JICA Open series, fourth
- Trophy de Pomposa JICA winner

2000 FORMULA A KARTS
- World No 1
- World Cup champion
- European champion
- Winner of Elf Masters

2001 FORMULA SUPER A KARTS
- World Championship, 15th

BRITISH FORMULA RENAULT WINTER SERIES with Manor Motorsport

Starts	Poles	Wins	Fastest laps	Rank
4	0	0	0	5th

2002 BRITISH FORMULA RENAULT with Manor Motorsport

Starts	Poles	Wins	Fastest laps	Rank
13	3	3	4	3rd

FORMULA RENAULT EUROCUP with Manor Motorsport

Starts	Poles	Wins	Fastest laps	Rank
4	1	1	1	5th

2003 BRITISH FORMULA RENAULT with Manor Motorsport

Starts	Poles	Wins	Fastest laps	Rank
17	11	10	9	1st

BRITISH FORMULA 3 with Manor Motorsport

Starts	Poles	Wins	Fastest laps	Rank
2	0	0	0	n/r

2004 FORMULA 3 EUROSERIES with Manor Motorsport

Starts	Poles	Wins	Fastest laps	Rank
20	1	1	2	5th

2005 FORMULA 3 EUROSERIES with ASM

Starts	Poles	Wins	Fastest laps	Rank
20	13	15	10	1st

2006 GP2 with ART Grand Prix

Starts	Poles	Wins	Fastest laps	Rank
21	1	5	7	1st

2007 FORMULA 1 WITH McLAREN-MERCEDES

Race	P1 pos	P2 pos	P3 pos	Qual pos	Laps led	Race pos	Champ pos	Points margin
Australian GP	4	3	3	4	4	3rd	3rd	-4
Malaysian GP	3	9	1	4	2	2nd*	3rd	-4
Bahrain GP	3	2	1	2	4	2nd	3rd	0
Spanish GP	1	5	1	4	8	2nd	1st	2
Monaco GP	2	3	3	2	5	2nd	2nd	0
Canadian GP	2	3	1	1	67	1st	1st	8
United States GP	3	2	3	1	66	1st	1st	10
French GP	6	4	1	2	0	3rd	1st	14
British GP	1	4	4	1	15	3rd	1st	12
European GP	1	2	2	10	0	9th	1st	2
Hungarian GP	5	3	3	1	70	1st	1st	7
Turkish GP	4	1	1	2	1	5th	1st	5
Italian GP	3	2	2	2	0	2nd	1st	3
Belgian GP	2	2	4	4	0	4th	1st	2
Japanese GP	4	1	20	1	55	1st*	1st	12
Chinese GP	4	4	3	1	24	Rtd	1st	4
Brazilian GP	5	1	2	2	0	7th	2nd	-1

* denotes set the race's fastest lap

- Lewis is also the youngest driver ever to lead the world championship
- Lewis is the first driver to finish his first nine grands prix on the podium. No new driver had ever managed more than their first two appearances on the podium
- Lewis was the first driver to lead at least a lap in more than their first five grands prix. He did it in his first seven. Juan Manuel Fangio held the previous record, at five
- Lewis is the first driver to score points in his first nine grands prix. Sir Jackie Stewart held the previous record, at six

The publishers would like to thank the following sources for their kind permission to reproduce the pictures in this book.

LAT Photographic: 97, 121; /Lorenzo Bellanca: 85; /Bloxham: 22; /Charles Coates: 79, 80, 82, 87, 91, 94, 98, 122, 128; /Chris Dixon: 25, 32, 34; /Glenn Dunbar: 11, 12, 42, 47, 48, 55, 58-59, 60, 64, 73, 77, 84, 102; /Jakob Ebrey: 44, 52, 53, 63; /Steve Etherington: 4-5, 69, 70, 72, 75, 89, 90, 106, 115; /Andrew Ferraro: 2, 61, 62, 76, 88, 108, 111; /Malcolm Griffiths: 105; /Andre Irlmeier: 50, 54, 56, 57; /Steven Tee: 7, 66-67, 74, 81, 86, 92-93, 101, 112, 117, 118-119, 124-125; /Terry/Ebrey: 45

PA Photos: /Hermann J. Knippertz/AP: 30-31; /Sutton Motorsport: 14-15, 21, 26, 35, 36, 38-39, 41, 46, 49

Rex Features: 28, 29; /Anglia Press Agency: 8, 17, 23, 27; /Philip Brown: 18, 24

Every effort has been made to acknowledge correctly and contact the source and/or copyright holder of each picture and Carlton Books Limited apologises for any unintentional errors or omissions which will be corrected in future editions of this book.